NF
Potter,

3

D1624001

92 1503

398.41
P
Potter
    Touch wood

DATE DUE			
	DISCARD		

398.41 POT
Potter, Carole.
 Touch wood

CLOC Library
Magnolia, Ark.

TOUCH WOOD

An Encyclopaedia of Superstition

92 1503

TOUCH WOOD

An Encyclopaedia of Superstition

Carole Potter

MICHAEL O'MARA BOOKS LIMITED

CLOC Library
Magnolia, Ark.

For my father who always believed that being the seventh son of the seventh son made him special; and for my mother who believes in *all* superstitions, just in case.

Published 1990 in Great Britain by
Michael O'Mara Books Ltd
9 Lion Yard
11–13 Tremadoc Road
London SW4 7NF

Copyright © 1983 by the Sammis Publishing Corporation

All rights reserved. No part of this publication may be
reproduced, stored in a retrieval system, or transmitted,
in any form or by any means, electronic, mechanical,
photocopying, recording or otherwise, without the prior
permission of the publishers. Such permission, if
granted, is subject to a fee depending on the nature of
the use.

A CIP catalogue record for this book is available from the
British Library

ISBN 1-85479-076-5

Printed and bound in Great Britain by
Redwood Press Ltd, Wiltshire.

INTRODUCTION

A SUPERSTITION

—A superstition is a belief or a notion which attempts to fathom the unfathomable, based on neither reason nor fact; sometimes it disregards evidence.

—A superstition is a way to get through a tough situation; it's a set of rules to follow in a game without rules.

—A superstition is a blindly accepted belief which probably dates back thousands of years and has outlived its original meaning and use.

—A superstition takes the fear out of the unknown.

—A superstition is something we think will change our luck.

Some superstitions were designed to help us see into the future, and who doesn't want to know what's ahead for us? And some evolved out of the fear of retribution. If, thought ancient man, we are basically unworthy of the gifts of the gods, then a little bit of luck might come in very handy. So, we'll thank the gods, we'll not tempt them by calling their attention to something wonderful, and we'll touch wood to keep the evil spirits away and to thank the good spirits for answering our prayers.

If you believe in not walking under a ladder, never inviting
thirteen to a dinner party, tying a red ribbon to a baby carriage and
never going back for something you've forgotten; if you always throw
salt over your left shoulder after having spilled some on the table, or
say *gesundheit!* when a friend sneezes; if you are terrified of black
cats and cross your fingers for luck; if you wear a charm around your
neck or read your horoscope each morning; if you do all of these
things, or even some of these things, you're in good company. Most
people believe, as Goethe did, that superstitions are "the poetry of
life."

Above all, a superstition is something never to be questioned
because you will find, as I did, that all superstitions are flawed, albeit
highly romantic, contentions. A superstition then, is an unswerving
belief that helps make life a tiny bit easier. And what's so terrible
about that?

> *Alas! you know the cause too well;*
> *The salt is spilt, to me it fell;*
> *Then to contribute to my loss,*
> *The knife and fork were laid across:*
> *On Friday, too! the day I dread!*
> *Would I were safe at home in bed!*
> *Last night (I vow to Heav'n 'tis true)*
> *Bounce from the fire a coffin flew.*
> *Next post some fatal news shall tell:*
> *God send my Cornish friends be well!*
>
> *(John Gay, 1700's*
> *Fables: The Farmer's Wife and the Raven)*

TOUCH WOOD

An Encyclopaedia
of Superstition

ABRACADABRA

See also AMULETS

This word, which we've all said dozens of times in jest, was taken very seriously during the Middle Ages. People believed that the word itself was a cure for fever. A sufferer would wear a parchment amulet around the neck with the word written in an inverted pyramid (in itself a magical symbol, *see* PYRAMID):

ABRACADABRA
ABRACADABR
ABRACADAB
ABRACADA
ABRACAD
ABRACA
ABRAC
ABRA
ABR
AB
A

In some parts of the world, it was believed that a person with fever simply had to write the word several times, each time dropping one letter as shown in the pyramid above. As the letters disappeared so would the fever. The charm was also believed to be helpful against toothaches and infection.

Belief in this magical word probably dates back to the centuries before Christ, but the exact name of the demon or evil spirit it comes from has been lost to history. By the second century A.D. the cabalists, an extreme sect within the Hebrew religion, were using a form of Abracadabra as a charm against evil spirits: *A*, meaning Father; *Ben*, Son; and *Ruach Acadach*, the Holy Spirit.

There was a belief common in ancient times that the mere name of a supernatural being held magical powers. People would evoke a name for protection—as we do today—and they felt that knowing the true name of the proper deity would be a help. Abracadabra became a term in the art of magic as this trend became more popular and the magicians began to use fantastic, incomprehensible words in place of the names of gods. The more obscure the words, thought the magicians, the more magical the powers.

ACHILLES' HEEL

If an arrow struck your heel, it would no doubt be very painful— but would it be fatal? A legend, which has been handed down to us by the Greek poet Homer, tells of a warrior known for his excessive bravery, strength, and most of all, invulnerability. In Homer's tale, Achilles' mother dreamed that her son would be killed in battle. To protect him, she bathed him in the River Styx, which coated him with a protective shield everywhere except on the heel by which she held him. It is said that during the Trojan Wars Paris shot Achilles with a poison arrow, guided by the hand of the god Apollo, which struck his heel and immediately killed the otherwise invulnerable warrior.

Medicine has honored Homer by naming the muscle connecting the calf to the heel the tendon of Achilles.

In today's idiom, any vulnerable spot in a person (or a system) is called an "Achilles' heel."

ACORN

See also OAK TREE

The little acorn, from which the famous great oak grows, has been worn as an amulet since the days of the druids. Druids held particular store in the oak tree and hence the acorn, which represented good luck and long life.

In Asia Minor, the acorn was sacred to the goddess of nature. The Scandinavians believed that the great god Thor, god of thunder, protected the oak tree. They believed that placing an acorn near a window would prevent lightning from striking the dwelling.

Today, some people still strongly believe that an acorn placed on a windowsill will protect them. A dried acorn is also often used as a windowshade pull.

Folklore gives additional significance to the acorn. Since it takes a very long time for an oak to grow from an acorn, the acorn is a symbol for a difficult achievement that has taken a lot of hard work to accomplish.

ALBATROSS

Consider the jinxed albatross. Imagine the horror of Coleridge's ancient Mariner:

> *'God save thee, ancient Mariner!*
> *From the fiends, that plague thee thus!—*
> *Why look'st thou so?'—with my cross-bow*
> *I shot the albatross.*
> (*The Rime of the Ancient Mariner, I*)

It is believed, mostly by sailors, that to kill an albatross is to bring bad luck to the ship and to everyone on it, and death to the person who killed it. An albatross that follows a ship is supposed to carry the soul of a drowned sailor in order to be near his mates. It is also believed that it follows to aid rescuers in case of a shipwreck.

Some think that an albatross sleeps while it flies because its flight seems motionless. Others believe that if the bird flies around a ship bad weather will continue for many days. Looking at a storm at sea, any captain might say, as the ancient mariner did:

> *Instead of the cross, the Albatross*
> *About my neck was hung.*
>
> *(II)*

ALL SAINTS' DAY (ALL HALLOWS)

See HALLOWE'EN

ALMOND

To the Victorians, the almond was a symbol of stupidity, indiscretion, thoughtlessness, and the impetuousness of youth. They reasoned that since the almond tree blossomed so early in the spring, it left itself wide open to frosts and other damage due to the fickleness of the weather. If the "stupid" almond tree had just waited until later in the season, it could have borne many more blossoms.

The significance of the almond goes back much further in history. The Greeks had a legend about it (indeed, the Greeks had a legend for almost everything). In this story, young Demophon, returning from the Trojan Wars, is shipwrecked and meets a Thracian princess, Phyllis. They fall in love and arrange to marry, but before the ceremony can take place, Demophon learns that his father has died in Athens and he must return for the funeral. He promises to return on a certain date but miscalculates how long it will take him, returning three months later than planned. By this time Phyllis, certain that he will never return, has hanged herself.

The gods, moved by her love, transform her into an almond tree. Demophon is distraught and offers a sacrifice to the almond tree, declaring his undying love. In response, the almond tree blossoms. Impetuous youth and undying love were thus symbolized by the almond prior to the Victorian Age.

Pliny advised in *Natural History*, in 77 A.D. that eating five almonds would prevent drunkenness. He also asserted that if foxes ate almonds with water, they would die.

In the sixteenth century pills containing ground almonds were made for travelers to take, in case they found themselves without food or water.

The Moslems mixed the paste of the almond with mother's milk as a cure for trachoma.

Today, the branch of an almond tree is often used as a divining rod. (*See* DIVINING ROD)

AMETHYSTS

Cleopatra wore them and so did Catherine the Great. Saint Valentine is said to have had one with Cupid's face carved upon it. Egyptian soldiers wore them into battle for a tranquilizing effect in dangerous situations, to insure victories. Perhaps the most wonderful thing about amethysts is the ancient belief that they prevented drunkenness! Greeks in early times believed that the amethyst, which is a wine-colored stone, prevented the wearer from becoming drunk, and so they named it *amethystos*, meaning "not to be drunk." They also carved drinking cups from amethyst to prevent the drinker from becoming intoxicated.

There is a Greek legend about Bacchus, god of wine and revelry, who was angry with the goddess Diana and swore vengeance upon the first mortal he saw. That happened to be a young maiden named Amethyst who came to worship at Diana's altar. When she saw Bacchus's tigers about to pounce on her she called to Diana for help. Diana instantly changed Amethyst into a statue to protect her. Bacchus, as a gesture of contrition, poured wine over the statue, making Amethyst a beautiful grape color and granting her immunity against the narcotic effects of the beverage.

In the Middle Ages, the gem became known as the Bishop's Stone because it was used in the ring a bishop wore on the third finger of his right hand to indicate that he was married to the Church.

For the Hebrews, the amethyst was the stone of Dan, one of the twelve tribes of Israel and stood for judgment, courage, and justice.

Amethyst is the stone of those born under Aquarius and is thought to encourage moderation and self-discipline in all Aquarians who wear it.

The February born will find
Sincerity and peace of mind;
Freedom from passion and from care
If they the amethyst will wear.

(ANON)

Some people believe that an engraved amethyst has extra powers. One engraved with the moon or sun could provide protection against storms. Amethysts with other engravings are thought to protect against drunkenness and thieves, insure pleasant dreams, or keep a wandering husband faithful.

If all this isn't enough, the amethyst is supposed to help against headaches, toothaches, and gout!

AMEN

Why say "amen" before and after prayers? It is believed that a loud, forceful amen, said in unison by worshippers, will keep open the doors of Paradise.

Amen is a sign of agreement, of affirmation, of approval, as the Book of Deuteronomy says,

All the people shall answer
and say Amen.

Macbeth, who probably needed the gates of Paradise to open before him more than most people in history, said:

I had most need of blessing, and 'Amen'
Stuck in my throat.

(Shakespeare, *Macbeth*, II:2)

AMULETS

See also ABRACADABRA
FOUR-LEAF CLOVER
HORSESHOES
RABBIT'S FOOT
TALISMAN

An amulet is an object used mostly to protect a person against evil, or to bring good luck. It can be worn, nailed to a front door, or fastened onto an automobile or baby carriage. An amulet must be a natural item, not man-made, and it may be anything the owner believes has special powers.

An amulet can be a ring, a stone, a book, a horseshoe, or a part of an animal. Probably the most popular amulet in history has been the rabbit's foot. (*See* RABBIT'S FOOT) Parts of animals are very popular amulets and are considered to be especially powerful in bringing good luck. A lion's tooth might be worn for courage; a tiger skin or a bear claw represents strength. In the fifties kids hitched foxtails to their bikes to insure speed.

Bells used as amulets are supposed to frighten away evil spirits and are often seen attached to oxen or horses for their protection. They were once considered very important amulets for travelers. Who knew what dangers lurked in a foreign land?

Golden objects are supposed to bring good luck because gold was believed to be made from the tears of the sun god. Heart-shaped amulets could provide the wearer with lasting love, as well as protection from heart disease.

One of the most popular amulets in Italy is the red pepper. A natural, dried red vegetable is still believed to keep the Devil away, because red is a color that frightens the Devil. (*See* CHARTS, COLORS) When a red pepper dries it resembles the Devil's horn. It is believed that it will keep you safe from his grasp. The protection of this particular amulet, however, has been greatly diluted in recent years because of the commercial manufacture of red plastic peppers. Can you imagine the Devil being afraid of a piece of plastic?

Other popular amulets include coral, mandrake root, four-leaf clover, human hair, teeth, representations of the human hand, medals of saints, birthstone rings, and abracadabra.

The difference between an amulet and a talisman is that an amulet is a passive thing—all you do is wear it. A talisman requires some involvement from the person seeking good luck. You have to kiss, touch, or wave a talisman in order for it to be effective. (*See* TALISMAN)

ANGELS

See STARS

ANKH

The ankh (pronounced like "tank") is a cross-like symbol that comes from ancient Egyptian hieroglyphics and means life. It was held in the hands of the pharoahs and by the various deities and is often translated as their "key to life."

The ankh is not thought to have any special mystical powers today. It regained some of its popularity, however, when author Jacqueline Susann used it in her best-selling novel *The Love Machine*. Consequently it took on explicit sexual connotations.

Another interpretation of the ankh, found in early Greek writings, is the Greek letter *tau* (T) which represents life; topped by a circle, which represents eternity, it implies eternal life.

In any case, the ankh has become an attractive talisman (*See* TALISMAN) which people wear on chains or as a ring.

APHRODISIACS

See also MANDRAKE ROOT
OYSTERS
TOMATOES

By and large, natural aphrodisiacs are a question of mind over matter. Shakespeare, in *Henry IV*, Part I; II:2, wrote: "I am bewitched with the rogue's company. If the rascal have not given me medicines to make me love him, I'll be hanged."

In ancient Rome, chicken soup was considered an aphrodisiac; in ancient Egypt lettuce was supposed to do the trick. Tomatoes (and potatoes) were once considered such strong aphrodisiacs that they were illegal. (*See* TOMATOES)

The word aphrodisiac comes from the name of the goddess Aphrodite, mother of Eros, from whose name we get the word erotic.

The ancients had a strong and abiding faith in the principle of like makes like. In other words, they felt that foods that resembled sexual organs would increase sexual pleasures. For example, asparagus and celery resembled the male organ; oysters (*See* OYSTERS) and clams, the female organs. In the same vein of like makes like, eggs and caviar are thought to be stimulating. (Unfortunately, there is some evidence that this power-of-suggestion school of sexual therapy works in reverse for as many people as it helps. There are many who won't eat these foods for the same reason that others gobble them!)

The botanist Nicholas Culpeper and other herbalists considered the artichoke to be under the influence of Venus. In 1649 he referred to artichokes and said, "Therefore, it is no Marvel if they provoke Lust." (*The Complete Herbal and English Physician Enlarged*)

APPLE

An apple a day keeps the doctor away. (Old English proverb)
To eat an apple without rubbing it first is to challenge the Devil.
(Old English proverb)
A bad woman can't make good applesauce (it gets mushy).
(Old English proverb)

The apple is a favorite means for finding future husbands: Give one twist of the stem for each letter of the alphabet and wherever it breaks is the first initial of your true love.

> *Apple peel, apple peel, twist then rest,*
> *Show me the one that I'll love best.*
> *Apple peel over my shoulder fly,*
> *Show me the one I'll love 'til I die.*

There is a wonderful Scandinavian legend that tells the secret of the gods' eternal youth. They munched on magic golden apples supplied by Idhunn, child of the supreme goddess, Frigga.

The Bible is strangely quiet on the subject of the apple. The fruit with which Eve tempted Adam may not actually have been an apple after all. The Book of Genesis just refers to the fruit of the tree, and the poor apple has taken a bum rap ever since. The apple tree was thought to be the tree of life and knowledge, and the apple remains a symbol of temptation.

The Greeks thought the apple stood for immortality. The Arabs believed it had curative powers. Almost all the English-speaking peoples believed in its magical qualities; and of course, it was used to prove Newton's Law of Gravity.

Perhaps the most famous legend regarding the apple is the American folktale of Johnny Appleseed. (*See* JOHNNY APPLESEED)

Folklore uses for apples abound, such as this sixteenth century proverb:

> *He that will not a wife wed,*
> *Must eat a cold apple when he goeth to bed.*
> (Thomas Cogan, *The Haven of Health*)

APPLE A DAY KEEPS THE DOCTOR AWAY, AN

See APPLE

APPLESEED, JOHNNY

The legend of Johnny Appleseed is based on fact. It tells of John Chapman, an eccentric and deeply religious man who roamed the American frontier planting apple trees and nurseries wherever he went. He encouraged the use of the name Johnny Appleseed and even referred to himself that way. He is often called the "American Saint Francis."

Chapman was born in 1774 and turned up in Pennsylvania around 1797. For the next forty-eight years he moved around the frontier, a bearded, hermit-like figure, barefoot and dressed in rags, with a sack of seeds slung over his shoulder.

> *Let all unselfish spirits heed*
> *The story of Johnny Appleseed.*
> *He had another and prouder name*
> *In far New England, whence he came,*
> *But by this title, and this alone,*
> *Was the kindly wanderer loved and known.*
> (Elizabeth Akers Allen)

APRIL FOOLS' DAY
(ALL FOOLS' DAY)

> *April prepares her green traffic light*
> *and the world thinks Go*
> (Christopher Morley, *John Mistletoe*)

But is all as it seems? The world may indeed burst forth in all its greenery—but is it only "contriving a lie for tomorrow," as Jonathan Swift tells us?

In earlier times in France, people were easily tricked in April into thinking that summer had arrived. People who were fooled were thought to be as green as the new grass after a long winter's hibernation. The most popular custom during the month was to send people on a "fool's errand."

The Roman myth concerning Proserpina, who was snatched by

Pluto, the king of the Underworld, to be his bride, provides another popular explanation of April Fools' Day. Ceres, goddess of agriculture and the mother of Proserpina, went running in vain after her daughter when she heard Proserpina screaming during the abduction. This, say some, began the custom of sending gullible people on a "fool's errand." It might also have been starting with Noah sending the dove from the Ark on a fruitless mission.

Most likely the modern customs of April Fools' Day started around 1752, when the Gregorian calendar was adopted in England and the New Year's celebration was changed from the week of March 25 to April 1 to January 1. Practical jokers continued to make calls and bring gifts on the old holiday, April 1.

> The first day of April,
> You may send a fool wither you will.
> (Fuller, *Gnomologia* #6135, 1732)

AQUARIUS

See also ZODIAC

Aquarius is the sign of the Water Bearer. The Egyptians believed that the Nile overflowed every time the Water Bearer dipped his bucket into the river, producing fertile crops. Aquarius became a symbol of the thirst for knowledge and the desire to impart that knowledge to others.

This is the sign of people born between January 20 and February 18. Aquarians are ruled by Uranus and Saturn, and are supposed to be innovative, unconventional people who love human nature. They tend to be undependable, interesting, courageous to the point of irresponsibility, enthusiastic, inventive, and though lovable, often erratic in love.

Wednesdays are good days for Aquarians. The numbers eight and four often work for them, and pastel blues and greens are their best colors.

Aquarians like to write letters, find aviation interesting, and should be careful to eat properly. The amethyst is the birthstone of the Aquarian. (See AMETHYST)

Some famous Aquarians are Franklin Delano Roosevelt, Ronald Reagan, Adlai Stevenson, Marian Anderson, and Paul Newman.

> *'How is your trade, Aquarius*
> *This frosty night?'*
> *'Complaints is many and various,*
> *And my feet are cold!'*
> *said Aquarius.*
> (Robert Graves, *Star Talk*)

ARIES

See also ZODIAC

Aries, the sign of the Ram, is the first constellation of the zodiac because of a very ancient myth that the world was created when the sun entered the sign of the Ram. In mythology, the Ram is often pictured lying on its side, gazing admiringly at its golden fleece.

Aries is the sign of people born between March 21 and April 20. These people, influenced by the Ram, are supposed to possess violent tempers and often die violent deaths.

Tuesdays are good days for Aries people, seven and six are their lucky numbers, and red is their best color. The birthstone for Aries is the diamond. They are ruled by Mars and so are assumed to possess courage. Since theirs is a fire sign, they are enthusiastic enough to inspire other people. They are reputed to be independent people, to be delighted by challenge, and to be good leaders with an ability to plan and develop effective programs.

Aries people are always taking risks. They are extravagant and have strong willpower, good constitutions, and a positive attitude. They are supposed to be difficult to love. Some famous Aries are Robert Frost, Marlon Brando, Nikita Khruschev, Bette Davis, and Tennessee Williams.

ASTRONOMERS' SIGNS FOR THE SEASONS

Spring   *Summer*   *Autumn*   *Winter*

Some Other Astrological Symbols:

Venus   *Earth*   *Mercury*   *Mars*

BABIES

First a son, then a daughter,
You've begun just as you oughta.

(Unknown)

If you rock a cradle while empty,
Babies you'll have a plenty.

(Unknown)

Monday's child is fair of face
Tuesday's child is full of grace
Wednesday's child is full of woe
Thursday's child has far to go.
Friday's child is loving and giving;
Saturday's child works hard for a living
But the child that is born on the Sabbath Day
*   is fair and wise, and good and gay.*

(Bray, Traditions of Devon)

When you have one,
You can get up and run,
When you have two,
You can go, too.
When you have three,
Better stay where you be
When you have four,
You go no more.

(Unknown)

Ever step over a crawling infant only to be yelled at and told you'll stunt the baby's growth, or been advised to carry a baby to the top of the house before bringing it downstairs for the first time? (It is said that if you have no stairs, you'll get the same good luck by standing on a piece of furniture with the child, or even on top of a box.)

Superstitions about what to do before the birth of a baby are probably as important as those about after it is born. Some, for example, are:

Babies born at midnight can see ghosts.
If your child is born while the moon is on the rise, it will be a girl.
A child carried high is sure to be a girl, and one carried low, to be a boy.
To make certain it's a girl, put a frying pan under your mattress; to insure that it's a boy, place a knife under the mattress.

More examples:
To cut the pain of childbearing, put an ax under the bed.
Mothers-to-be should not witness ugly events because children are marked by what their mothers see, hear, and do during pregnancy.
The sins of the fathers are visited on the sons.
A pregnant woman should always eat the foods she craves or the child will be born with a birthmark in the shape of that food. (How about a chocolate chip cookie?)

Once your child is born, be sure to:
brush the baby with a rabbit's foot; (See RABBIT'S FOOT);
put a coral necklace around its neck; (See CORAL);
present the child with a fresh egg, a pinch of salt, and a loaf of bread;
make certain the baby sneezes (See SNEEZING) to rid itself of evil spirits.

Don't:
   let the baby look in a mirror (*See* MIRROR) before it is a year
      old;
   cut the baby's fingernails (*See* FINGERNAILS) before a year—
      the mother must bite off the growing nails, or the child will
      grow up to be a thief.
   let a cat into the room. (*See* CAT)

Whichever of these superstitions you choose to heed or ignore, the result will still be a splendid child. At least that's what Charles Dickens promised in *Nicholas Nickleby*: "Every baby born into the world is a finer one than the last."

BACHELOR'S BUTTON

The lovely little blue flower known as a bachelor's button has always been associated with love and marriage. During Victorian times it was the flower most favored by young men in love.

The Orientals believe that the flower could foretell a happy marriage. They say that the flower should be picked early in the morning, then placed in the young man's pocket and not looked at for twenty-four hours. If it is still fresh and "true blue" the next day, the couple will have a good marriage. If, on the other hand, it has withered (which is highly likely after twenty-four hours in someone's pocket), then the marriage plans must be terminated. That seems to agree with the Italian proverb that says, "Praise all wives, but remain a bachelor." After all, this way of choosing a bride does seem to have all the odds stacked against it.

Throughout history the word bachelor has implied a novice as well as a man who has never been married. Originally a bachelor was a kind of cowhand. The word might have come from the Latin *baccalarius*, one who cares for cows. The meaning changed during the Middle Ages. Bachelor then referred to a young knight who was serving as a vassal to a member of the gentry.

During modern times it has meant "a man who hasn't been caught yet." If the man lets the bachelor's button make his decision for him, he'll "never get caught."

BAKER'S DOZEN

See also THIRTEEN

A baker's dozen has always meant thirteen items instead of twelve. The phrase goes back as early as the 1500s, and Rabelais included it in his writings. (*Book V*, Chapt. 22)

There are two schools of thought about its origin. One is that when retailers bought their dozen loaves of bread to resell to the public, they got an extra loaf free as a commission. But it is more likely that in earlier times a baker included a thirteenth loaf with every twelve to avoid being accused of short-weighing the bread.

BANANA

The banana is a food some people use to wish upon. Make your wish, then eat your fruit—or cut a slice from the stalk end of the fruit while making a wish. In either case, if you find a Y-shaped mark at the end your wish will come true. (I haven't the faintest idea why.)

BANSHEE

Wailing like a banshee is to be making an unearthly sound to foretell a death in the family. In old Gaelic tradition a banshee was a household spirit, usually a beautiful woman, who took particular interest in the well-being of the family. When death was near, she let out an unholy wail which could be heard throughout the county. Today the woman is usually a hag. In either guise, the banshee's most valuable asset is her ability to foretell death.

BARBER'S POLE

The wonderful candy-striped pole in front of the local barber's shop dates back to fifth-century Rome, when barbers were also surgeons. They treated wounds, pulled teeth, and bled patients.

The white in the pole represents bandages; the red, the blood. Attached to many poles in early England was a brass basin, which represented the bowls used to catch the blood during letting. Barbers performed bloodletting chores right through to the sixteenth century.

Ultimately surgeons took over their rightful practice and the brass bowl began to disappear from the barber's pole. The red and white stripes remain.

BAR MITZVAH

In the Jewish religion, the Bar Mitzvah is a ceremony during which a thirteen-year-old boy assumes the responsibilities of manhood and the responsibilities of his religion. The custom did not begin until the fourteenth century, although writings imply that some sort of symbolic celebration was held when a male reached puberty in ancient times.

The boy, in a loud, clear (and usually high-pitched) voice proclaims, "Today I am a man!"

BATS

There is a popular belief that the Devil, when he isn't doing something to bother people, takes the shape of a bat. Some people believe that the bat is a familiar (a familiar is the servant of a witch). Some believe that ghosts take the form of bats and therefore houses with bats in them are haunted.

To the Chinese and the Poles, bats are a good omen. The Chinese say that bats fly with their bodies down because their brains are so heavy and also believe that the bat is the symbol of long life and happiness.

In most other countries, bats are thought of as evil things. To the Irish, the bat is a symbol of death. There is a common idea that if bats move into a house, the occupants will shortly move out (sounds like common sense to me).

Did you know that the heart of a bat—dried, powdered and

carried in a front pocket—will turn a bullet or stop a man from bleeding to death; and if you wash your face in the blood of a bat, you will be able to see in the dark?

Another superstition that many believe is that if a bat lands on your head, it will not leave until it hears the thunder of an approaching rainstorm.

Incidentally, expressions such as blind as a bat and bats in the belfry indicate that we once knew very little about bats.

BATS IN THE BELFRY

See BATS

BEARDS

See also HAIR

> *Beware of that man, be he friend or brother,*
> *Whose hair is one color and beard another.*
> (Unknown)

> *The properness of a man lives altogether in*
> *the fashion of his beard.*
> (Anonymous, *Humor Out of Breath*, 1608)

> *A red-bearded man was never any good.*
> (*German Proverb*)

> *Beware of women with beards,*
> *And men without them.*
> (*Basque Proverb*)

In 350 B.C., Alexander the Great ordered his troops to shave so that the enemy would not be able to grab them by the beard in order to more easily decapitate them.

Beards have always been an especially important symbol. A beard was a mark of wisdom and was associated with a man's soul. The beard became a symbol of masculinity early in history because young boys and eunuchs had neither body hair nor virility.

The beard also became an almost holy object. People reasoned that since the beard continued to exist even after having been shaved off, it was intended by the gods to always be there.

To the ancients hair, like fingernails, eyelashes, and other nonpermanent parts of the body (*See* FINGERNAILS) were considered pieces of the person never to be discarded. If they fell into the wrong hands the person's soul was in deep trouble. It was unlucky to cut your beard for fear the Devil would get hold of the clippings. Whenever hair was clipped it was immediately burned as a precaution.

The beard is even today so important to the Moslems that they take their oaths by the beard of the Prophet Muhammad; and Orthodox Jews consider it sacred. In ancient Greece, men with beards were commonly considered philosophers. In fact, the ancient Greek word *pogonotrophos* meant "man with a beard" which was synonymous with philosopher.

The beard has been a royal status symbol for centuries. In ancient times, beards of iron were tied with ribbons or straps to the chins of kings and even queens, as depicted in hieroglyphics found on the tombs of Egyptian rulers. The boy king Tutankhamen, for instance, usually had a glorious black beard attached to his chin.

Long ago Egyptians and Babylonians used curling irons and dyes on their whiskers, and at festival times they indulged by using perfumes and powders on their beards. The kings of Persia were known to intertwine their beards with gold.

Women with facial hair have never been popular. As late as the fifteenth century women with hairy warts or chin hairs were condemned as witches and often burned at the stake.

Cleanshaven faces became the rage in Elizabethan England because the queen decided to tax all Englishmen who wore beards!

In *Adagia* (1523), Erasmus wrote, "Since the beard is not completely formed until the age of manhood, it has always been considered an emblem of wisdom." In recent decades beards have become more a symbol of rebellion than of maturity and wisdom.

BEES

Bee venom is an ancient cure for rheumatism, arthritis, and other joint diseases that is even more popular today. The venom, in the form of a cream, can be bought in health food stores and pharmacies throughout the world. In ancient times the treatment was more complicated than simply rubbing in a cream. It involved submitting to two bee stings on the first visit and one at each subsequent visit.

One ancient idea is that bees were messengers to the gods and kept them informed of what was happening among mortals—the local gossip column, so to speak. Later, bees were seen as gods' spies. "Wisdom of the bees" and "ask the wild bee for what the druids knew" are two expressions that probably come from this idea.

The Irish talk to bees all the time, and many people believe that if they don't tell the bees when someone dies, the bees will stop making honey.

A bee flying into your house is supposed to mean that a stranger is coming.

It's good luck if a bee flies into your house, then leaves, but it's bad luck if it dies in your house. It's also bad luck if a swarm of bees comes at you of its own accord, even if this happens only in a dream.

BEETS

In 1649 an herbalist named Culpeper wrote in *The Complete Herbal and English Physician Enlarged* (1649) that beets were good for headaches and colds and helped clean out the liver and the spleen. Some believe, even today, that eating a raw beet each day will keep cancer away.

The Greeks themselves left no record about their use of beets, but we do know that they served them on a silver platter to the great god Apollo in his temple at Delphi. Dare we assume that what was good enough for Apollo was good enough for his subjects?

BEGINNER'S LUCK

See GAMBLING
   LUCK

BELL, BOOK, AND CANDLE

The expression bell, book, and candle is actually from a solemn form of excommunication in the Roman Catholic Church. It is more symbolic than religious. When the sentence of excommunication is pronounced—

> *A bell is rung*
> *The book is closed*
> *A candle is extinguished*

—this indicates the spiritual darkness to which the person has just been condemned.

The phrase is also used to indicate that someone is a witch, since being a member of the Church and being a witch are incompatible.

BELLS

See AMULETS
   BELL, BOOK, AND CANDLE

BEST FOOT FORWARD

See also RIGHT SIDE OF THE BED

Put your best foot forward is an expression that dates at least to the time of Shakespeare, who had King John declare (in *The Life and Death of King John*, IV:2): "Nay, but make haste the better foot before."

BEST MAN

See WEDDING CUSTOMS

BIRDS

> *A bird in the Hand is worth two in the Bush*
> (Plutarch, *Of Garrulity*, third century B.C.)
>
> *A little bird told me.*
>
> (Ecclesiastes 10:20
> and Jonathan Swift, *Letter to Stella*, 1711)

The relationship between humans and birds is special, ancient, and in some places revered. It was believed that birds could talk and that certain people could understand them. When a wise man learned to imitate birds he could inform a gullible audience that "a little bird told me" whenever his wisdom was questioned.

Birds were thought to be messengers of departed souls. When a bird tapped on a window or flew into a house, it was assumed that a spirit was in search of another to join it; in other words, it was a messenger of death. From this belief came at least two important superstitions:

If a bird flies into the house, an important message will follow.
It's unlucky to have wallpaper with birds on it in your home.

White birds especially are, to some, a sign of death. Blue jays are also special. They are thought to spend every Friday with the Devil, telling him about the bad things we've done all week. Whenever a blue jay is seen flying overhead carrying twigs he is thought to be bringing fuel to the fires of Hell.

The Mohammedans believe that no bird can be trusted because birds opened the gates of Paradise and let the Devil enter.

You must listen very carefully to tell where a birdcall is coming from, because:

From the north, it's for tragedy
From the south, good for crops.
From the west, good luck will be
From the east, good love.

BIRTH

See BABIES

BIRTHDAY CAKE

Thanks to the Greek goddess Artemis, the goddess of the moon, we have such things as birthday cakes. Artemis's birthday was celebrated with moon-shaped honey cakes with candles on top.

Holy books from many religions say that if a phrase is written upon a piece of food, and the piece is eaten, the person will gain the power in the phrase. Thus we say, "Happy Birthday!"

The superstition connected with birthday cakes actually has to do with the candles: Blow them all out on your first puff and you'll get your wish.

BIRTHDAYS

See also BIRTHDAY CAKE

Celebrating birthdays dates to ancient times, when man first began to understand the stars. It became important to know the exact moment, day, month, and year, of one's birth. With these all-important facts, a horoscope could be drawn, and in those days a horoscope was essential.

The Egyptian pharaohs celebrated their birthdays in a big way. Back then the amount of celebrating a person did generally had to do with the extent of his or her money and power. Rich Romans held circuses.

We know that Cleopatra and Nero enjoyed their birthdays, as did most Romans and Greeks. Augustus held a birthday celebration for himself every month!

Good wishes are offered to the birthday person in an attempt to protect him or her from evil spirits. The chances of spirits causing mischief on a birthday are considered great, because spirits of all kinds are said to be attracted by celebrations and by times of change, and this dangerous combination comes together at birthday time.

The birthday celebration dates to recorded time. The modern party probably started in early Germany, where children were given gifts and had a candle-rimmed cake. (See BIRTHDAY CAKE)

Birthday customs changed a lot after Christ was born. Children were named after saints and celebrated the birthday of the saints after whom they were named instead of their real birthdays. Today many children celebrate both days.

The idea of someone "worth his weight in gold" comes from a birthday tradition in the East. For example the Aga Khan III on his sixtieth birthday topped the scales at 243 pounds and received that amount in gold and diamonds.

One of the best birthday ideas comes from China. There people once believed that when a person reached the age of sixty, he or she got to start all over again.

BIRTHMARKS

See also CHARTS, Language of the Mole

A mole on the back of the neck is a sign that the person will be hanged.
(Old English Proverb)

The birthmark, like so many other omens and symbols, has contradictory meanings. It is called the mark of God; it is also called the mark of the Devil.

In fact, birthmarks are unexplained changes in skin pigmentation. But those who believe they are bad luck think they are evil enough to cause cancer, and those who believe they are good luck charms go so far as to throw black pepper on an expectant mother so that her child will be born with birthmarks. Other beliefs are:

More moles on the left side than the right is bad luck.

Oblong moles are bad luck.

If you've got a mole above your chin
You'll never beholden to any of your kin.

The Greeks thought birthmarks were good; and centuries ago, they developed the Language of the Mole as an expression of their love toward those women born with these dark marks. During the decades moles have gone in and out of fashion, and at times a woman was considered inelegant without one.

During the late nineteenth century, women often wore patches like moles called beauty spots, in various shapes and sizes. Depending upon where she put it, a woman could say something special to the men who admired her. For example, a very proper young lady might have worn a beauty patch to indicate that she wanted to be left alone!

A mole on your arm
Can do you n. harm.
A mole on your lip
You're witty and flip.
A mole on your neck
Brings money by the peck.
A mole on your back
Brings money by the sack.
A mole on your ear
Brings money year by year.
(Old English rhyme)

BIRTHSTONES

See also AMULETS
CHARTS, Birthstones

The concept of birthstones probably dates back six thousand years. The Egyptians believed that such stones protected them from

disease, poisoning, and other calamities. The tomb of the High
Priest of Memphis, (from 4,000 B.C.) was found to contain a breastplate with twelve different stones, which were probably amulets
worn for protection against the evil spirits in the afterworld.

The idea of birthstones has evolved from that breastplate to the
charts now often written on greeting cards. The Egyptians passed
their beliefs on to the Hebrews, who assigned a stone for each of the
twelve tribes of Israel. These were passed on for the twelve angels of
Paradise. Later the stones became the twelve foundations of the
Apostles and finally became symbolic of the twelve months of the
year. Something that took so long to evolve shouldn't be taken too
lightly! Check your birthstone in the CHARTS section, and get
yourself a birthstone amulet, quickly.

BITE YOUR TONGUE

See also CHARMS
          COUNTERMAGIC

When someone tells you to bite your tongue they are suggesting a
countercharm. They don't want what you've just said to come true
and they hope the evil spirits haven't heard it.

If you've been lying, or exaggerating outrageously, someone
might well say to you "bite your tongue," so that the lie or the
exaggeration doesn't come true.

BLACK

See also BLACK CAT
          BLACK FOR MOURNING
          CHARTS, Colors

> *Though I am black,*
> *I am not the Devil.*
> (George Peele,
> *Old Wives Tale*)

Black was the color of death; the color of all things dark, unknown, and often deadly; therefore, it was evil personified.

Some good things are associated with black: It is the color of fertile earth, which ancient civilizations worshipped. It is the color of dignity, elegance, and sophistication. The Egyptians believed that black cats (*see* BLACK CAT) had divine powers.

To the Japanese, black was the color of the soul as it left the body. Both the early Christians and the Cherokee Indians believed it represented death. For the Hindus, it is the color of Siva, the Great Destroyer.

Early African legend tells how people became black by eating the liver of the first ox killed.

Perhaps the first blacklist was Henry VIII's roster of monasteries whose lands he greatly desired to confiscate.

Both the Jolly Roger (the flag of pirates) and the flag of Hitler's SS troops, was black, with a skull and crossbones.

BLACK CAT

See also CAT

It's hard to know which superstition about black cats came first. There is the Norse legend that tells of the chariot of the goddess Freya, which was pulled by black cats. (When the Norse people were converted to Christianity, Freya became a witch and the black cats became black horses—which were uncommonly swift and undoubtedly possessed by the Devil.) The legend goes on to say that after seven years of service as horses, the cats were rewarded by being turned into witches—disguised as black cats.

In ancient Egypt, where cats were revered above all other animals (*See* CAT), the black cat was a lucky symbol. But by the Middle Ages, when notions of witchcraft started running rampant, black cats began to take the rap for everything bad. The black cat was believed to be the mascot or the familiar of witches; and as in the Norse legend, after seven years' service, to become a witch itself. If a black cat crossed your path it was a sign that Satan had been taking notice of you.

Because of its long association with witches, the black cat is the symbol of Hallowe'en. (*See* HALLOWE'EN) It is said that these possessed creatures perch on sleeping babies and old people and suck the breath out of them.

Sailors like black cats, and sailors' wives keep them to insure their husbands' safe return.

> *If the cat in your house is black,*
> *Of lovers you will have no lack.*
> (Anonymous)

Good luck will come your way if a strange black cat comes to visit. It turns to bad luck when the cat decides to stay.

In America a black cat crossing your path is bad luck. In England a black cat walking toward you is good luck. In Japan a black cat crossing your path is good luck. Take your pick!

BLACK FOR MOURNING

See also WIDOW'S PEAK

In ancient times, it was thought that death was contagious. It was also believed that some deaths were caused by neglect in some way, and so evil spirits could easily get into the dead body. Mourners wanting to be as inconspicuous as possible wore black, in the belie that it was less likely to attract the attention of death.

This belief was fairly widespread. People were afraid of ghosts and tried to hide light skin under the black cloth of mourning. In some primitive societies people even painted themselves black; in Afric people often painted themselves white for funeral ceremonies.

The custom of wearing black for mourning is not universal:

In China and Japan they wear white.
In Egypt and Burma they wear yellow.
In South Africa they wear red.
In Ethiopia they wear light brown.
In Syria and Armenia they wear violet.
In Iran they wear light blue.

In America it used to be customary to wear black for six months when mourning. The length of time has gradually dwindled to a few weeks or even days.

BLACK FRIDAY

See FRIDAY
      WITCHES AND WARLOCKS

BLARNEY

There are two perfectly wonderful tales about Cormac MacCarthy, the lord who built Blarney Castle, near County Cork, in Ireland. Take your pick.

In the fifteenth century, MacCarthy was embroiled in a lawsuit, which he was sure to lose. He appealed to the druid princess Cliodna, who told him to kiss a stone of the castle and that "words will pour out of you." He did, and they did, and he won his lawsuit. He then moved the stone to an inaccessible spot so that everyone could not get at it and turn Ireland into a country of con artists.

The other story has MacCarthy Mor, lord of the castle, losing a battle to an Englishman named Sir George Carew. MacCarthy agreed to surrender to the British, but each day he put them off with another excuse. Finally Queen Elizabeth I herself tried to get him to surrender, but all she got in return was a long-winded, evasive letter to which she is said to have replied, "This is more of the same Blarney!"

The Blarney stone itself is a limestone triangle, which is supposed to be so difficult to reach that anyone who can hang from his or her heels to kiss the stone will be eternally charming and persuasive.

BLIND AS A BAT

See BATS

BLONDES

See HAIR COLOR

BLUE

See also CHARTS, Colors

Children say:

> *Touch Blue*
> *And your wish*
> *Will come true.*

Brides look for something blue to wear for their wedding ceremonies. (*See* WEDDING CUSTOMS) The pharaohs wore blue for protection. A saying goes: "Wear beads of blue, keep danger far from you."

Blue was the color that protected people against witches simply because witches don't like blue: It's the color of Heaven.

> *If your love for me is true,*
> *Send me quick a bow of blue.*
> *If you ever of me think*
> *Send me quick a bow of pink.*
> *If you have another fellow*
> *Let me have a bow of yellow*
> *If your love for me is dead,*
> *I'll know it if your bow is red.*
> (Unknown)

The name Bluebeard evokes an image of a murderous husband, and the blues referred to the "po' man's heart disease."

BLUE MOON

A blue moon isn't impossible, it's just rare. Once in a blue moon doesn't mean never, just not very often.

A blue moon is a result of certain atmospheric conditions that cause the moon to appear blue. This is an astrological oddity, but it happens.

The Egyptians liked the color blue and felt it was a lucky color. They were especially partial to what they called the "thirteenth moon," which their astrologers usually made blue because it completed the astrological cycle with a lucky sign.

BREAD

There are so many superstitions connected with bread that it's a wonder it ever gets eaten. An early idea was that bread was a gift from the gods, never to be eaten without a word of praise. The saying of grace before eating (which comes from the Jewish prayer said over bread) is a symbolic holdover of this idea.

That bread must be broken, not sliced, comes from the same concept: It would be an insult—indeed harmful—to cut the bread since it was a gift of God.

The ancients believed that there were four elements to life:

> Water—stream of life
> Grain—the fields
> Earth—sustenance
> Sun—goodness

Each of these elements are found in bread, "the staff of life." To pass the bread among friends was to wish them a long and healthy life.

Remember:

> It's bad luck to cut bread from both ends.
> Never pass bread around on a knife or a fork.
> Never leave a knife stuck in a loaf of bread.
> If you toast on a knife you'll be poor all your life.
> It's good luck to dream of bread.
> When two people reach for the same slice of bread, company is
>   coming.

The heel of a loaf is always reserved for a member of the family because it means good luck.

A loaf of bread turned upside down means death or a ship in trouble. (Some think this superstition comes from the legend of an English general who, centuries ago, gave the signal to attack the Scots by turning a loaf of bread upside down.)

BREAK A LEG

See THEATRICAL FEARS

BREAKING GLASS

See WEDDING CUSTOMS

"BREAD AND BUTTER"

Ever walk with a friend and have a tree, a park bench, or another person come between the two of you—then hear your friend mutter, "bread and butter"? It's a common superstition that something else will come between the two of you to end your friendship, unless you quickly say "bread and butter" and cross your fingers.

Saying "bread and butter" is a symbolic way of uniting the two parts of a whole, just as bread and butter go together to form a complete unit.

There are other things to do that are supposed to prevent friendships from breaking up, but this is considered the most effective and certainly the most popular.

BRER RABBIT

Brer Rabbit, along with Brer Wolf, Brer Squirrel, and other animals of the forest, belongs to a group of tales told by Uncle Remus to a small white boy who is enchanted by the humanlike creatures.

These are all characters in stories written by Joel Chandler Harris. Harris was a white man who grew up on Southern plantations and never forgot all the tales he heard from the blacks who worked the land, or the impact the stories made on him and on the black children who listened with him.

The Uncle Remus stories recall the African tradition of humanizing animals. They also serve as an allegory of slavery: The powerless rabbit is victorious within his own "neck of the woods." Brer Rabbit (probably "Brother Rabbit" in Southern dialect) is the "cunningest critter in the forest" and always outsmarts Mr. Man. *Uncle Remus and His Friends, Old Plantation Stories, Songs, and Ballads with Sketches of Negro Character,* by J.C. Harris, are the sources of this imaginative story.

BRIDAL BOUQUET

See WEDDING CUSTOMS

BRIDE

See WEDDING CUSTOMS

BRIDESMAIDS

See WEDDING CUSTOMS

BRIDGES

Since bridges are man-made structures, built to circumvent nature, many superstitions have grown up around them. For example: while driving under a bridge, if a train passes overhead, put your right hand against the roof of the car and make a wish.

It is also believed that if you say good-bye to someone while standing on a bridge, you will never see that person again.

Here's my favorite: If you make a wish at one end of a bridge, then close your eyes, hold your breath, and navigate your way to the other side, your wish will come true. (On the other hand, you could fall off the bridge and drown!)

BROKEN HEARTED

Long ago, people thought that the feeling produced by over-stimulation of the emotions (a rapid heartbeat), meant that the heart was breaking. Don't you believe it!

BROKEN MIRROR

See MIRROR

BROWNIES

See SMALL FOLKS

BRUNETTES

See HAIR COLOR

BUCKEYE

See CHESTNUT

PAUL BUNYAN

The legend of Paul Bunyan, America's most famous logging hero, is based on pure fiction. James MacGillivray used the name Paul Bunyan in tales of his own youth as a backwoodsman around 1910. The advertising executive W. B. Laughead took that figure and made him into the larger-than-life hero we think of today, by using him in an advertising campaign for Red River Lumber.

The legend of Paul Bunyan began to grow, and this fictional character took on a quasi-real background. It was said that Bunyan was born in Maine and that his cradle, too big to remain on land, was floated on the river—every time the giant baby turned, he caused a tidal wave. Once, when the baby was sleeping so soundly he couldn't be wakened, the British Navy was called in to help. The sailors spent seven hours shelling the giant in an attempt to wake him. When finally he did awake, he stood up, and in so doing sank seven warships!

Lore takes Bunyan on to Minnesota and Wisconsin with his ox, Babe, who could haul 640 acres' worth of logs at one time. Paul's crew, all giants, ate in a legendary way: It was said that they ate pancakes and biscuits so big that when a biscuit dropped, an earthquake occurred on the other side of the world!

BURIAL BEHAVIOR

See CEMETERY
    DEATH CUSTOMS
    WAKES

BUTTERCUP

The buttercup might have gotten its name because cows that feed on buttercups give yellower milk. A lunatic may be cured by merely hanging a cloth bag holding the flowers around his or her neck. Herbalists believe that an ointment made from buttercups should be used to draw a blister.

Buttercups are mainly used to tell if a friend is honest, angry, or in love. The test works this way: Hold the flower under your friend's chin, and if the yellow from the bloom shines on the skin then everything your friend says is true. The same reflection can indicate that the friend is angry or in love—or even jealous. It's difficult to decide. You might have to ask your friend what he or she is feeling!

BUTTONS

See also AMULETS

In ancient times buttons were worn strictly as ornaments, until, in the thirteenth century, someone was clever enough to invent the buttonhole. Buttons predate the buttonhole by perhaps fourteen hundred years.

Buttons were thought to be good luck when given as a gift. They were worn as amulets after being exchanged among friends.

Black magic has its own uses for buttons—particularly black ones. If someone thinks that an illness is caused by an evil spell, then the sick person must leave a black button where someone else can find it—thus passing on the illness.

In the United States kids say:

> *Rich man*
> *Poor man*
> *Beggarman*
> *Thief*
> *Doctor*
> *Lawyer*
> *Merchant*
> *Chief*

as they count their buttons, to see which profession will be theirs or which profession their spouses will have.

In England, the rhyme is a little more complicated:

> *Tinker, tailer, soldier, sailor*
> *Gentleman, apothecary,*
> *Plowboy, thief.*
> *Soldier brave, sailor true*
> *Skilled physician, Oxford blue*
> *Learned lawyer, squire so hale*
> *Dashing airman, curate pale.*
> *Army, Navy,*
> *Medicine, Law,*
> *Church, Nobility,*
> *Nothing at all.*

This version of the rhyme takes a lot of buttons.

Finally, there's the common superstition that if you put your button in the wrong buttonhole, bad luck will follow you all day long. To stop such evil goings-on, take the piece of clothing off and start all over again.

CANCER

See also ZODIAC

There is a legend that the Crab, the symbol for Cancer, bit Hercules and was rewarded by one of the warrior's enemies, who made the Crab into a constellation in the sky. Astrologers believe that when the sun is in Cancer, any storms that occur will be catastrophic. People who are born between June 21 and July 22 are Cancers.

Cancers are ruled by the moon. They tend to be homebodies and are often oversensitive in their relationships with other people, causing great emotional problems for themselves. Cancers are highly emotional about most things. They are warm and giving, but sometimes too overwhelming as lovers. They withdraw when criticized and eat when depressed. People go to Cancers with their troubles because they are often sympathetic and kind.

Cancer, the crab

Fridays are good days for Cancers. Eight and three are their lucky numbers; and silver and white are their good colors. Their birthstone is the ruby.

Cancers love to entertain at home. They are torn between their home and possessions and leaving for some new adventure. Those who are friends with Cancers find them tenacious and stubborn— traits they get from the Crab.

Famous Cancers are Louis Armstrong, Nelson Rockefeller, Neil Simon, Ernest Hemingway, James Cagney, and Lena Horne.

CANDLES

To understand the importance of candles in the world of superstitions, one has to understand something about evil spirits. Whenever people are having fun, whenever there is an important occasion of any kind, evil spirits are going to come to help you celebrate whether they are invited or not. An evil spirit isn't likely to come into a brightly lighted room. It prefers dark, intimate places. Throughout most of history, candles were the only means of lighting. They became all-important for keeping evil spirits away from happy events.

In Ireland, people light twelve candles in a circle around a dead body, as double protection: Evil spirits can't cross into a circle (*see* CIRCLES), and they are deterred by the lighted candles.

A couple of ideas that have grown up around the original association of evil spirits and candles:

A blue light from a candle indicates good spirits nearby (or ghosts).

When a candle goes out during a religious service, evil spirits are lurking in the corners.

Wax candles are used in church because bees come from Paradise. (*See* BEES)

Candles are very big in witchcraft and voodoo. A candle can be used as a voodoo doll. To call a lover, for instance, stick two pins through the candle. Then say this little incantation:

> *It is not this candle alone I stick*
> *But my love's heart I mean to prick.*
> *If* (name) *be asleep or* (name) *be awake*
> *I'll have* (name) *come to me and speak.*

By the time the candle burns down to the pins, your lover should have arrived (it didn't work for me).

CANDLEMAS DAY

See GROUNDHOG DAY

CAPRICORN

See also ZODIAC

Capricorn, the sign of the Goat, is one of the oldest constellations of the zodiac. It is governed by Saturn. People born between December 22 and January 19 are Capricorns.

Capricorns are practical, reliable, conservative, and above all ambitious. They tend to have an insatiable appetite for success. Saturn makes them both frugal and ambitious for power, and their symbol, the Goat, allows them to make great sacrifices in pursuit of their goals.

Capricorns appear cold, even snobbish. Those who know Capricorns well, however, find in them great inner resources of love and affection. Capricorns make highly responsible leaders, with a realistic if not pessimistic outlook. They should eat hot, invigorating foods; they tend to be melancholy but are good in a crisis.

Saturday is a good day for Capricorns. Seven and three are their lucky numbers, and dark green is their color. Their birthstone is the garnet.

Capricornus, the goat

Some famous Capricorns are Muhammad Ali, Marlene Dietrich, Howard Hughes, Benjamin Franklin, Carl Sandburg, Richard Nixon, and Joan of Arc.

CARNATIONS

There is a legend that the carnation is known as a flower of rejoicing because it was first seen on earth at the birth of Christ. This idea is very romantic, but there is evidence that the flower existed prior to the birth of Christ.

During those centuries, in fact, it was believed that the carnation could preserve the human body and keep away nightmares. Some also believed it grew at the graves of lovers, and it became popular in funeral wreaths. Others said it cured melancholy. Pliny the Elder wrote in *Natural History* that carnations were used to spice various drinks.

The carnation is the flower of those born in January. It stands for fascination and a woman's love (*See* CHARTS, Victorian Language of Flowers). Carnations may be worn on Mother's Day (*See* MOTHER'S DAY): A white carnation indicates "in memory"; a red one, "in honor of the living."

In Korea they believe the carnation can tell important things about a person's future. If a cluster of three flowers on a single stem is placed in the hair and the top flowers die first, the last years of life will be hard; if the bottom one dies first, there will be bad luck early in life; and if they all die together then the person is in for trouble throughout life.

CAT

See also BLACK CAT
THEATRICAL FEARS

If a cat crosses the street it is a sign of bad luck.
(Aristophanes, *The Ecclesiazusae* 393 B.C.)

The cat, as an object of worship, had its heyday around 3000 B.C. The Egyptians worshipped the cat-headed goddess Bast, the protector of pregnant women. This goddess enjoyed music, dancing, and the good life. When a cat died in ancient Egypt it was mummified and buried in Bast's temple. The law in those days said that when a household cat died, the members of the family had to shave their eyebrows and mourn. Killing a cat, even accidentally, was a capital offense.

In ancient Burma and Siam it was believed that a holy man's spirit entered a cat after his death; when the cat subsequently died, the holy man's spirit went to Paradise.

Now you have to admit that even with all the love and attention modern cats get, they are not *that* well off. Then again, it was rougher for cats during the Middle Ages, when witchcraft blossomed and cats were thought to be the Devil incarnate. (*See* BLACK CAT)

To straighten out some old wives' tales: Cats do not have eyes that shine in the dark, nor can they see in the dark. They do not suck away the breath of sleeping children, or invalids, although they do like to snuggle close and examine the human face. The idea that they suck away breath comes from beliefs about witchcraft in the Middle Ages. (*See* BABIES) The idea of being "nervous as a cat" is also erroneous—cats aren't nervous; they merely have good reflexes.

Some other superstitions are:

A restless cat means a storm is brewing.
When a cat licks its tail, rain is coming.

If you throw a cat overboard, there will be a storm at sea.
Never kick a cat or you'll get rheumatism.
Never drown a cat or the Devil will get you.
If a cat meows on board ship, it will be a difficult trip.
It's good luck to have the family cat at your wedding.
In New England they say they can tell time (and tides) by the
   pupils of a cat's eyes.
When a cat puts its tail toward the fire, bad weather is coming.
When a cat licks itself clean, it means fair weather, rain, or
   company.
If a cat jumps over a corpse, the corpse will become a vampire.
   You must stop the funeral immediately and wait until the cat
   has been caught and killed. (Since killing a cat is also bad
   luck, you can't win when this happens, no matter what you
   do.)

CEMETERY

See also DEATH CUSTOMS

One of the crying needs of the time is for a suitable burial
service for the admittedly damned!

(H.L. Mencken, *Prejudices*, Sixth Series)

These are things that *should not* be done when near a cemetery:
   Pointing at a grave (it will make your finger rot).
   Counting the cars of a funeral procession.

Here's what you *should* do:
   Bury your loved one on the south side (it's holier ground).
   Try to pick a rainy day—then the departed spirit will go to
   Heaven.

Whenever you shiver it means someone is walking over the spot
where your grave will be.

CHAMPAGNE

See WINE

CHARMS

See also ABRACADABRA
AMULETS
BITE YOUR TONGUE
EVIL EYE
TALISMAN

Charms are mostly chants recited by priests and other believers. They are thought to bring good luck or protect against bad luck when used with words or gestures.

The term good luck charm, when applied to tangible things, is inaccurate. Those are good luck amulets or good luck talismans. (*See* AMULETS; TALISMAN) Modern usage, however, permits all three terms to be used.

An example of a charm used for burns:

> *Two angels came from the west*
> *One brought fire,*
> *The other frost.*
> *Out fire, in frost.*

CHESTNUT (BUCKEYE)

Got a backache; a headache; pain from rheumatism? Then carry a chestnut. Chestnuts, boiled with honey and glycerine, are supposed to cure asthma and other chest problems. (Oh that old chestnut!)

On Hallowe'en (*See* HALLOWE'EN) chestnuts are always left on the table for any souls of the dead who come back to visit on that night.

CHILDREN

See BABIES

CHRISTMAS

See also HOLLY
          MISTLETOE

Although Christmas is a celebration of the birth of Christ, it might have had some connection with the Birthday of the Unconquerable Sun, which was a holiday celebrated by the Romans in ancient times to honor the sun god.

There are several superstitions and traditions which surround the Christmas holiday. For instance:

Christmas morning—The first person through the door of a household must be a man. (In olden times groups of men would go from house to house carrying the image of Christ, to insure that a man was the first to cross the threshold.)

Christmas decorations—All must be down by January 6 (Epiphany) or bad luck will follow all year.

Gifts—Although we think that gift-giving at this time of the year started with the gifts of the Magi, it actually started much earlier, during the Roman holiday that commemorated Saturn and the planting of the seeds. This period was also a day of equality, when Roman rulers abdicated their control and the "elected" peasants ran the land.

Santa Claus—The jolly fellow with the red suit and whiskers who climbs down chimneys was introduced by Thomas Nast in a series of Christmastime cartoons which ran in *Harper's Weekly* from 1863 to 1866. Santa Claus was based on Saint Nicholas, who has been traced to Asia Minor around 350 A.D. The feast day for Saint Nicholas was December 6, and gifts were exchanged on that day. Saint Nicholas was combined with Kris Kringle, a nineteenth-century German creation who brought gifts for the children. Kris Kringle was a corruption of the Christ Child, the original gift bearer of German legend.

Christmas cards—Sending cards at Christmas was a custom introduced in the 1840s by John Calcott Horsley. It didn't become popular in the United States until a printer named Louis Prang took up the idea and marketed the cards, making a bundle of money for himself and creating havoc for the postal service.

Christmas carols—The Christmas carols we know today come mostly from the 1800s. Caroling, however, was an old English custom; it means to sing joyously.

Christmas trees—There are several stories about the possible origin of this custom. There is a legend that Saint Boniface, a missionary who worked among the German druids, was cutting down an oak tree (*See* OAK TREE) that was holy to the pagan druids and found hidden behind the oak a lovely little evergreen tree. More modern legend concerns Martin Luther, who is supposed to have used an evergreen tree to illustrate to his wife and children how wondrous he thought the winter night sky was. He put candles on the tree to indicate the stars.

Poinsettia plants—This is a relatively new custom. Dr. Joel Poinsett, a United States minister in Mexico, first brought back the plant in 1828 after hearing a story about a little Mexican boy who was too poor to put a gift into the poor box on Christmas Eve. The boy prayed outside of the church and on the spot where he knelt a beautiful red plant bloomed. The boy immediately gave the plant to the statue of the Christ Child. In Mexico the plant is known as *Flor de la Noche Buene*—"Flower of the Holy Night."

Feasting—Turkey has been a favorite at Christmastime for a long while. In an 1890 publication, *Statesmen's Dishes*, the following recipe was found by Robert Myers in his "Celebrations":

> *To prepare a turkey for Christmas dinner: the tur-*
> *key should be cooped up and fed well sometime before*
> *Christmas. Three days before it is slaughtered it should*
> *have an English walnut forced down its throat three*
> *times a day and a glass of sherry once a day. The meat*
> *will be deliciously tender and have a fine nutty flavor.*

Eating mince pie dates from the Middle Ages, when the
Crusaders acquired a taste for exotic spices. The English
wassail bowl, which comes from an expression meaning "be
of good health," contains ale, roasted apples, eggs, nutmeg,
cloves, and ginger. Finally, there is the idea that the ab-
breviation Xmas is sacriligious. It isn't: It comes from the
Greek X, Chi. In earlier times, X–mas was used as a sacred
symbol because it associated the cross with the holiday.

CHRYSANTHEMUMS (MUMS)

The word chrysanthemum comes from the Greek for golden
flower. The chrysanthemum is considered a lucky flower for those
born in the month of November.
Although it was a popular flower in ancient Greece and Egypt, the
chrysanthemum was more important in China and Japan. It became
Japan's national flower. During the War of the Dynasty in 1357 (also
known as The Chrysanthemum War), each Japanese warrior wore a
yellow chrysanthemum as "a golden pledge of courage." For the
Japanese, the flower is the symbol of human perfection and the
ancient emblem of the Mikado. The coveted Order of the Chrysanthemum is the highest honor the Japanese can bestow.
In China, the flower and its images were considered sacred and
were used extensively in temples and in the decorative arts. A story
goes that there is a stream in China set in a bank of chrysanthemums,
and if you drink from that stream you'll live for one hundred years.
In ancient times the chrysanthemum was considered a symbol of
longevity and perfection. Drinking water with chrysanthemums was
supposed to prolong life.
The Chinese eat chrysanthemum petals in salad. The Italians use

it as an herb. The Koreans boil its roots to make headache cures. It is believed by some to be a good antidote for opium, vertigo, and melancholy. In New England, it was once used in church bouquets to help keep the congregation awake during long sermons.

CIRCLES

Superstitions about circles began in the very early days of the sun worshippers. It was believed that life and all eternity were ruled by the cycle of the sun, which was thought to move in a circle. People did things clockwise (east to west), the way the sun moves, to honor the sun. The expression "going around in circles" probably dates back to very early days.

It was believed that evil spirits could not enter a circle, since the circle represented the sun and the sun was all-powerful. The first use of lipstick also comes from sun worship. The mouth was thought of as the entrance to the body, and a red circle drawn around the mouth kept the soul inside—and the Devil outside.

Later, witchcraft took full advantage of this theory. Witches cannot cross into a circle, nor can outsiders get into a circle a witch has drawn for herself and her coven.

A powerful countercharm to bad luck is turning completely around in a clockwise direction three times. (*See* COUNTER-MAGIC)

CLERICAL COLLAR

See KNOTS

CLOCKWISE

See CIRCLES

CLOTHING

Centuries ago people believed they could outwit death by wearing their clothing inside out, as a kind of disguise. This led to our current belief that if you accidentally put a piece of clothing on inside out, and you leave it that way all day, it will bring you good luck.

If you get a new coat you had better put a coin in the right pocket to insure good fortune. Never have your clothing mended on you or you'll soon die (or more likely, your brains will be sewed up by the tailor). If you want to counteract these two dread possibilities, chew on a piece of thread during the whole operation.

COINS

See AMULETS
  MONEY
  WISHING WELLS

COOK ONE'S GOOSE

This expression, which means ultimately to ruin one's prospects, comes from the Middle Ages. There are two schools of thought about it, both involving King Eric XIV of Sweden.

Eric is supposed to have answered that he wanted to "cook your goose for you" when a town he was trying to capture asked about terms for a truce. The town, not sufficiently impressed by Eric's army, had hung out a goose for Eric's soldiers to shoot at.

The second version of the same legend is that the town had hung out the goose as an insult because the goose is such a stupid and futile creature. This gesture of contempt so angered Eric's army that it burned the town to the ground, effectively "cooking their goose" and ruining the town's prospects of victory.

COPPER BRACELETS

The miraculous curative powers of copper have been redis-covered by both the gullible and the desperate in recent years. In India, copper earrings are believed to ward off sciatica.

The belief that copper bracelets are a protection against the pain of arthritis and rheumatism started in the Middle Ages. Sending your money for a strand of copper to wear is sure to do only one thing—turn your wrists green.

CORAL

See also AMULETS

For many centuries people have worn pure, red coral as an amulet for protection against the evil eye. The Romans, and later the Italians, felt that coral effectively warded off demons and witches as well as the dread evil eye. (*See* EVIL EYE)

Coral is believed to prevent arguments in the home; hung on a bedpost it will prevent nightmares. The Chinese believed that it was protect against madness.

In the Middle Ages, ground coral that was crushed in a mortar made of marble was considered a medicinal aid for almost every ailment.

CORN (MAIZE)

Corn is a product of the Americas, and the legends surrounding it come from this part of the world.

Many Indians believed that the Great Spirit had invented corn during a famine and that anyone who wasted it was doomed to hunger.

There are many Indian legends which tell how corn came to North America. The following is typical of the genre:

A young warrior dreamt that a lovely yellow-haired squaw appeared to him and instructed him to burn a prairie covered by grass and then drag her by the hair across the burning fields. Each time he paused, new ears of corn sprouted, and on each ear a small tuft of the squaw's yellow hair grew. These tufts of hair were to remind the warrior that she would never forget her people.

CORNERSTONES

If you think your landlord wants his pound of flesh each month, he's only operating in accordance with the ancient assumption that the gods of the earth must be paid for their land. In the centuries before Christ, people paid for the privilege of building every new building or construction. The payment was in the form of a sacrifice, and more primitive peoples often offered children as payment.

As the custom evolved coins were placed within the walls of the structure as payment. This in turn became the use of a cornerstone to mark the beginning of the building and to bless the construction.

There is a superstition connected with cornerstone-laying ceremonies, which states that an unmarried woman shouldn't attend these ceremonies; if she does, she won't marry for another year. That's silly, but the initial reasoning behind the idea was sound: A virgin was thought to be the best sacrifice to the vengeful protector of the earth.

COUNTERMAGIC

When bad luck is unmistakably coming your way, there are some countercharms which, I am assured, work. Saliva is probably the best weapon. (*See* SALIVA) Spitting over your left shoulder, for instance, is supposed to usually work. Turning around three times (if the threat is very serious, seven times) often precedes spitting. (*See* CIRCLES) Turning around is an attempt to reverse the order of things, in this case to reverse the direction of the bad luck headed your way.

The other, reasonably effective thing to do is to pull your pockets inside out. (*See* CLOTHING)

It's also helpful, whenever in doubt, to cross your fingers. (*See* CROSS YOUR FINGERS)

CRACKED MIRROR

See MIRROR

CRICKETS

See also WEATHER

Almost everybody thinks the cricket is good luck. This is one of the few talismans that from ancient times on have been universally accepted as fortunate to have around. The cricket is a "house spirit" and brings good luck to the dwellers of a home. The cricket is also believed to take his luck with him; when he leaves the house, so does the luck.

The Japanese, the English, and the American Indians all believe in the inherent luck of this little creature. It is thought to be bad luck when he leaves by your chimney; it is terrible to kill one; it is also dangerous to imitate his chirp.

The cricket is a super fortune-teller and knows if rain is coming, if death is near, and even if a lover is coming back.

CROCKETT, DAVY

Davy Crockett always said: "Be always sure you're right, then go ahead." He was called the "coonskin congressman" and he told crowds he was "so ugly that his grin could bring a coon down from a tree."

Crockett, an American hero turned legend, was born in 1786 and served as a frontier scout under Andrew Jackson during the Creek Indian War. He was later elected to the U.S. Congress from Tennessee for three terms. After losing his congressional seat, Crockett fought in the Battle of the Alamo and became one of the few survivors of the battle, only to be shot by Santa Ana in 1836.

The legend of Davy Crockett was in large part perpetuated by Davy himself. He loved to repeat tall tales about himself, like the one where he shot 105 bears in eight months. He reveled in his reputation as a comic backwoodsman with homespun intelligence and unending courage. Because of Crockett we have the coonskin cap, a permanent part of the American wardrobe to be taken out every now and then and paraded in public.

CROSS-EYED

See also EVIL EYE
            RABBIT'S FOOT

Don't enter a card game with a cross-eyed partner—you're sure to lose.

If you meet a cross-eyed person of the opposite sex, you'll have good luck; but if you meet one of your own sex, that's trouble. To counteract this bad luck, spit through your fingers and outstare him or her.

CROSSED KNIVES AND FORKS

See KNIFE AND FORK

CROSSES

See also ANKH
            CROSS MY HEART AND HOPE TO DIE
            CROSS YOUR FINGERS

The sign of the cross as an emblem for a religion, an individual, a country, or as a signature, has been used since the beginning of human time. By the time Christ was crucified on the cross, it had been a symbol for centuries.

Some of the more popular forms of the cross are indicated above.

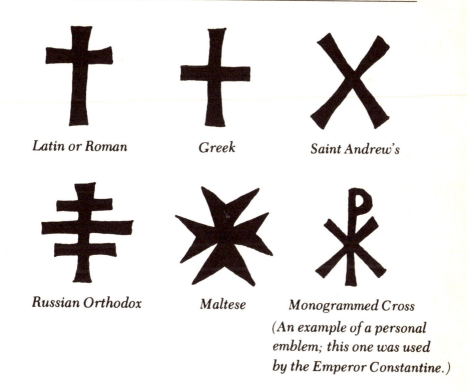

Latin or Roman   Greek   Saint Andrew's

Russian Orthodox   Maltese   Monogrammed Cross
(An example of a personal
emblem; this one was used
by the Emperor Constantine.)

CROSS MY HEART AND HOPE TO DIE

When you cross your heart (and hope to die) while making the sign of the cross with the index finger of the right hand, you are obviously telling the truth.

Long before Christianity, the cross was a sacred symbol. Since it was assumed that the heart was the seat of all wisdom, it was believed that the heart would know if you were lying.

CROSS YOUR FINGERS

Crossing your fingers is the simplest way of making the sign of the cross. As a charm against the Devil, this sign is particularly effective. A cross has perfect unity: It represents the four directions, and the four elements.

When two lines cross, a wish (or a lie) can be held at the point where the lines meet. A wish will stay at the crossed point until it comes true; a lie will stay at that point, kept away from the evil spirits and from starting trouble.

In early times, two people crossed their index fingers together while the first person made a wish and the second hoped it would come true. This was later simplified into one person crossing his or her own fingers.

So, please keep your fingers crossed for me, will you? I'm hoping for my wish to come true.

CROWS

See also BIRDS
          SCARECROWS

There are several little rhymes that tell the story of the crow's place in the world of superstition.

> *One's bad luck*
> *Two's luck,*
> *Three's health,*
> *Four's wealth,*
> *Five's sickness*
> *Six is death.*
> (English saying)

> *One means anger*
> *Two means mirth*
> *Three a wedding*
> *Four a birth*
> *Five is heaven*
> *Six is hell*
> *But seven is the devil's own self.*
> (English saying)

Do you know the one about how the crow came to be black? The crow was originally white, legend says, but he turned black after eating snake eyes.

CUPID

> *This wimpled, whining, purblind, wayward boy,*
> *This senior-junior, giant-dwarf, Dan Cupid's*
> *Regent of love-rhymes, lord of folded arms,*
> *The anointed sovereign of sighs and groans,*
> *Leige of all loiterers and malcontents.*
> (Shakespeare, *Love's Labour's Lost III:1*)

Cupid, or Dan Cupid as he was often called, was the son of Mercury and Venus in Roman mythology and the god of love (known as Eros in Greece). Cupid, as the personification of love, stands for desire, passion, and all the problems associated with the affliction of this emotion.

Cupid is usually depicted as a beautiful, naked boy with wings, carrying a bow and arrow, and sometimes blindfolded. His arrows are supposed to shoot love through his targets.

The name Dan Cupid is another form of "Don Cupid"; don is a title meaning sir or master.

CURSES

See also CHARMS

Everyone curses; it's the way we wish evil onto others. Today when we curse someone, we usually don't mean it—and even if we do mean it, nothing usually happens. But there was a time when a curse was a very serious matter. Families were cursed in perpetuity; their cows couldn't give milk; chickens couldn't lay eggs.

To curse someone is to invoke the wrath of a great power against which the accursed has little protection. A curse is spoken magic; if you don't believe in magic, then a curse becomes blasphemous or meaningless.

DAISIES

"The smile of God" or "day's eye," as the daisy was called in ancient times, opens its white petals with the sun and closes them again at nightfall.

The centuries-old children's game of foretelling one's love life by pulling the daisy's petals and saying, "He loves me, he loves me not," was legitimized by Marguerite in Goethe's *Faust I* (1808).

In the Language of Flowers, the daisy means innocence; the common garden-variety daisy actually says, "share your sentiments," or "I reciprocate your attentions."

Knights in medieval times wore daisies into battle. It was widely known at the time that any knight using the double daisy (a stem with two blooms commonly found among garden daisies) as his emblem was declaring that he loved a lady and she loved him back. If, during those days, a lady couldn't make up her mind, she wore a wreath of white daisies to say "I'm not sure."

Wordsworth said that the daisy was "the poet's darling" (*To the Daisy*) because of all the romantic legends which have grown up around the flower. In sixteenth-century France there was an Order of the Daisy, and some say it was Mary Magdalen's tears that originally created the daisy.

Some common notions are:

> If you want to dream of your lover, put daisy roots under your pillow.
>
> Step on the first daisy you see or it will grow on your grave within the year.

92 1503

The spirits of babies who died at birth have scattered daisy seeds in abundance to help cheer their unhappy parents.

Medicinally, daisies are supposed to be very useful: If insane people drink a potion containing daisies for fifteen days, they'll be cured (or dead). As a charm, daisies cure wounds, gout, fevers, and ulcers, remove warts, and change gray hair to black. Daisies are also used as an ointment for eye infections. The juice of the English variety was once thought to cure migraines.

DANDELIONS

The dandelion is one of nature's purest diuretics and was known during the Middle Ages as "piss-a-bed." (A current superstition is: If you pick dandelions you'll wet your bed.)

In the sixteenth century the flower was called "lion's tooth" in England, and "dent-de-lion" in France, which later became anglicized to the current dandelion.

Known by children and lovers throughout the world as "love's oracle," the dandelion foretells romance when its puffball of seeds is scattered helter-skelter by someone blowing and reciting the eternal chant, "He loves me, he loves me not."

As a weather forecaster, the dandelion has limited use, but it is believed that if the flower doesn't open in the morning it will rain; and if it blooms in April and July, it will be hot and rainy throughout the summer.

The flower is thought to be good for the liver or against rheumatism, and to purify the blood. Dandelion juice is rumored to work as a tonic on any number of organs.

DEATH CUSTOMS

See also CEMETERY
        MOURNING VEILS
        WAKES

If you've wondered, as I have, why people are buried so quickly,

CLOC Library
Magnolia, Ark.

the reason is that ghosts shouldn't be encouraged to hang around too long.

A classic superstition about death and dead bodies is the notion of putting coins, or coppers, on the closed eyes of the deceased. People still do that today, for numerous reasons. Centuries ago, people thought that the soul left the body through the hollow eye sockets and since the Devil could enter that way, the coins were to close the holes. The Book of Genesis (46:4) says, "Joseph shall put his hand upon thine eyes," along the same lines. In classical Greece and Rome, the coins were payment to the god of the Underworld for his chore of ferrying the soul to the land of the dead.

Schoolbooks say that a doctor laid silver half-dollars on Lincoln's eyelids after he died—but then, he was the President. Most of the time the coins used are of copper.

Before someone dies:

> A dog will howl
> An owl will screech
> A picture may drop
> There will be a rapping sound at the window
> The sound of church bells will ring in your ears
> You'll see a falling star
> You'll dream of muddy water

—or any other of a thousand such signs; but there will always be a sign.

About cremation: An early idea was that evil spirits lived inside dead bodies and had to be burned. The Greeks, however, thought that by cremating the body the soul was liberated, and that the souls of buried bodies were outcasts and would probably never get to Paradise.

We know that in ancient Egypt mummification was the preferred burial procedure. The Egyptians believed that the dead spirit would return to the body, and it was preserved for future use.

The Romans didn't believe in an afterlife and didn't bother with mummification.

Today's tombstone is used to mark the site of a grave and to say the person's been in this world. Yesterday's tombstones were designed to keep in the ground the evil spirits that inhabited the dead body.

That was also the reason for the extremely thick, heavy coffins we see in museums.

Remember, in ancient times people firmly believed that death was contagious (*See* BLACK FOR MOURNING), and most of their efforts were to keep the dead from getting at the living and taking them away with them.

DEATHWATCH

This unhappy turn of a phrase refers to a species of beetle known as the deathwatch beetle, whose favorite pastime is tapping on wood. It is believed that if you hear that tap, there will be a death in your family.

Another explanation for the expression comes from the centuries-old tradition of waiting and watching for the ghost of a dead person to come back and cause trouble shortly after the funeral (*See* WAKES)—like Hamlet's father's ghost, who stirred up all those problems because he wouldn't stay dead and buried.

DEMOCRATIC DONKEY

See also REPUBLICAN ELEPHANT

In 1870, the popular *Harpers Weekly* cartoonist Thomas Nast drew "A Live Jackass Kicking a Dead Lion." The sketch, which showed a donkey kicking a carcass, had the U.S. Capitol building and the U.S. eagle in the background. The carcass was generally understood to be the Secretary of War Edwin M. Stanton and the donkey the treacherous Copperheads (the Northern backers of the Southern cause at the time of the Civil War).

The Democrats and other Copperhead opponents loved the cartoon. The donkey became permanently associated with the Democratic Party, even though it was used mostly as a sign of ridicule against them. The Democrats decided to use the donkey as their symbol and turn the ridicule to their own advantage.

The Democratic Party is like a mule.
It has neither pride of ancestry nor hope of posterity.
(Ignatius Donnelly,
Speech in the Minnesota Legislature, 1860)

DEVIL

The Devil and me, we don't agree;
I hate him; and he hates me.
(Salvation Army song)

An apology for the Devil—it
must be remembered that we have
only heard one side of the case.
God has written all the books.
(Samuel Butler, *Notebooks*)

Talk of the devil, and he'll appear.
(Erasmus, *Adagia XVII*, 1500)

The Devil is the Hebrew "Satan," the Old Testament's version of the archenemy of mankind. Translated into Greek Satan was *diabolos*, which means accuser, from *diaballein*, which literally means "to throw across" and in the idiom of the day meant to slander or accuse. The Devil means the accuser of the soul.

In Christian and other mythologies, the Devil is the fallen angel who became God's enemy. All evil is accredited to the Devil.

"To give the devil his due," a common expression, comes from *Don Quixote de la Mancha* by Cervantes.

Should you have an idea that you want to trade your soul with the Devil for some special wish, then the best time and place to meet him is at a crossroads at midnight.

DIAMONDS

See also CHARTS, BIRTHSTONES

A sixteenth-century writer once remarked that the diamond

makes the wearer unhappy because
its brilliance irritates the soul
just as an excess of sun irritates the eye.
(Jerome Cardan)

Of course, that's an irritation most of us don't mind, since the diamond is the most precious of gems.

The Persians believed that diamonds were sinful and an invention of the Devil. Some people believed that diamonds were the result of thunderbolts. In the Middle Ages, it was thought that two diamonds could produce a third.

As one of the most honored of gems, the diamond was regarded by the Romans as insurance for victory in battle when worn as an amulet on the left arm, and as protection against the evil eye for women of beauty if worn close to the face.

The stones have been considered lucky throughout history with the exception of very large diamonds, which have long and bloody histories. The extreme value of the stone added to the problems of keeping and wearing large diamonds.

Until recently, diamonds could only be cut by other diamonds. Today, the laser is used in industry for the cutting of this stone. It is completely false that diamonds cure leprosy and insanity and prevent nightmares. They are symbolic of virtue, purity, and innocence. They have also been proved effective as an amulet against the plague and against sorcery. The diamond is the birthstone for those born in April.

DIMPLES

It's the Irish who first said:

Dimple on the chin,
The Devil within.
Dimple on the cheek
A soul mild and meek.

Or:

A dimple on your cheek
Many hearts you will seek;

A dimple in your chin,
Many hearts you will win.

The ancients believed that people with dimples had special, magical powers, because so few had them. In more modern times, people believed that a man with a dimple in his chin or cheek would never commit murder. (Did you hear that, Kirk Douglas?)

Some people say that a dimple, in a smile, implies a loose character; but Shakespeare had a better idea. He claimed that "Love made those hollows" (*Venus and Adonis* L. 242).

DIVINING ROD

A divining rod is a forked branch, usually made of hazelwood or from a willow tree and is supposed to locate water and other minerals under the earth. It is also known as a dowsing rod.

The stick is said to dip in the presence of water. Many diggers, in fact, won't start a well unless the rod has indicated the right spot. This method of divining water is very old, but it is still widely used.

DOG DAYS

This does refer to the fact that dogs go mad, get fleas, and often howl during certain weeks, but that's not how dog days got their name. The dog days are those between July 3 and August 11 when the Dog Star Sirius rises with the sun, adding its heat to the sun's to produce the hottest time of the year. The Romans were the ones who named the period, calling that part of summer the "days of the dog."

There is a belief that it is an unhealthy time of year. (It might well have been for the Romans, who had no air conditioning.) There is no reason why it is considered unhealthy to swim during the dog days, although many mothers of (unhappy) children still believe that superstition.

According to legend, the flies increase, the rain seldom falls, dogs go mad, and snakes go blind and strike at any sound during the dog days.

DOGS

Love me, love my dog
(Ancient Latin proverb)

We say that some canines are good watchdogs; the Greeks in ancient times called them psychic. They were supposed to howl at approaching evil. Today, we credit a dog's sharp instincts and split-second reflexes for his ability to respond to danger. The Greeks, however, didn't understand those instincts and credited the dog with the power to see evil coming.

One legend suggests that howling dogs were a sign that the god of Wind had summoned death, and that the spirits of the deceased would be carried away because of the howling. Even today, many believe that a howling dog means someone will die, or that the dog has seen death and is howling at it.

The notion of the dog as a faithful companion or as "man's best friend" dates back to Homer's *Odyssey*. The dog, Argos, watched many years for his master, Odysseus (Ulysses), to return, and when Odysseus did, even though he was heavily disguised, Argos recognized him and, wagging his tail with joy, died of happiness (and old age).

DRAFTS

Hot or cold drafts are a sign that evil demons are in the air and are about to pull some nasty prank on good people. Even Kublai Khan believed that.

Many Europeans, Africans, and Americans believe that the warm air of a draft comes from Hell during a summer evening.

DREAMS

We are such stuff as dreams are made on.
(Shakespeare, *The Tempest* IV:1)

We all dream; what those pictures mean, and what causes a certain dream on a given night—that's a whole other kettle of fish.

Interpretations of dreams are different from place to place, and often from generation to generation, although judging by the bookstalls there are plenty of people who think they understand what it all means and can offer a simple list of explanations.

Dreams are as individual as the people who have them. The Romans and Greeks believed that dreams were warnings of future happenings, and the Egyptians thought the gods spoke through dreams. The Hebrews thought that dreams were very important, and often carried out their affairs according to the dictates of a dream. By the 1400s it was believed that "dreams go by contraries"—whatever you dreamed meant the exact opposite.

Edwin Radford, in his *Encyclopaedia of Superstition* (1949), gathers up a list of what many dreams are supposed to mean:

> Dreams of sickness mean marriage among young people.
> Dreams of angels indicate happiness coming quite soon.
> To have dreamed of standing before an altar implies sorrow and misfortune.
> Dream of being angry with someone special and that person will turn out to be your best friend.
> Dreams of fishing mean that for each fish you catch, a friend will die soon.
> Dreams of dancing indicate good fortune is coming.
> Dream that you've gone bald and you'll lose friends or property.
> A dream of a wedding means death.
> Dreams of bees or bee stings are very bad luck.
> Dream of fruit out of season and you'll wake up in tears.
> Dreams of marriage and brides always mean death and illness.

> *I believe it to be true that dreams*
> *are the true interpreters of our*
> *inclinations; but there is art*
> *required to sort and understand them.*
> (Montaigne, *Essays* III.13)

DROWNING PEOPLE COME UP THREE TIMES

When you see someone drowning, don't wait for the third time—because there might not be one.

Most drowning people rise because there is air remaining in their lungs (and other parts of the body) creating a buoyancy. Some people never rise back to the surface at all. Sometimes, if the person has some control during the crisis, he or she may rise several times before all the air is expelled. In this case three is not a lucky number.

DWARFS

See also: SMALL FOLKS

According to countless legends, dwarfs are good at blacksmithing and baking, at tailoring and at prophesy-making. They can disappear whenever they want, and they love to attend parties. They often give good advice, but they are known to be thieves and can't be trusted. Dwarfs are so very special, that any gift gotten from a dwarf may turn into a pot of gold.

Dwarfs are tiny, often misshapen people who, during early times, had their own kingdom, ruler, and laws. They dwelt in caves and were considered guardians of the minerals and precious metals found within the earth. The dwarf is a lucky symbol and an important character in mythology.

The main difference between dwarfs and other small folks is that dwarfs are real people—there are no leprechauns, are there?

DYBBUK

A dybbuk is the Jewish version of an evil spirit, the soul of a dead person, or a demon that takes possession of a healthy person and lives through that person. Leo Rosten, in *The Joys of Yiddish*, says that the idea of the dybbuk is as old as demonology, as old as man himself.

The dybbuk is a colorful, corrupt, and often vicious spirit that must be exorcised by a holy man who commands the spirit to leave the person and go to its eternal rest. It is believed that a tiny drop of blood remains behind on the small toe of the right foot to indicate that the spirit has exited the body. You'll also find a small crack in the window by which the spirit has left the room.

EAGLES

There is an ancient Egyptian belief that every ten years the eagle soars through the fires of Hell and then plunges into water and sheds its feathers, thereby acquiring a new life. (This is a good explanation of molting.)

There's another ancient legend that Adam and Eve didn't die but were actually turned into eagles and went to live on an island off the coast of Ireland. (Guess who thought that one up!)

Through the centuries the eagle has come to stand for strength and swiftness, and it was the emblem of many royal houses. The Romans began using the doubleheaded eagle when their empire merged with the Germans', joining their eagle to that of the Huns.

In folklore the eagle has always been a helpful bird, bringing warnings of trouble to the heroes.

EARRINGS

Throughout history, earrings have been effective amulets against the evil eye (*See* EVIL EYE) and were worn by both men and women. Kings, poets, and sailors all wore earrings for superstitious reasons. Sometimes only one was worn; sometimes two were needed.

Sailors believe that wearing earrings protects them from drowning, and that it helps their eyesight.

In ancient times the ear was thought to be the center of intelligence. The custom of pulling a child's ear to make him remember his school lessons comes from that ancient belief.

Earrings for men have come back in style in recent years. For some it's simply an ornament; for others it's a symbol of sexual preference.

EASTER

See also: EASTER EGGS
GOOD FRIDAY
RABBIT'S FOOT

Easter is the first Sunday after the full moon after March 21. According to Christian religion, it was the day that Christ was resurrected.

As with other Christian holidays, there was also a holiday in ancient times that was celebrated at about the same time. In this case, it was the celebration of the vernal equinox—the tribute to the goddess of spring, Eastre. Eastre was an Anglo-Saxon goddess who is reputed to have opened the gates of Valhalla for the slain sun god Baldur, thereby bringing light to man. Easter also refers to the rising of the sun in the east.

Some traditional Easter beliefs are:

The sun will dance as it rises on Easter Sunday.

It's good luck to wear new clothes on Easter Sunday in honor of nature's new green clothes.

The Easter lily is a symbol of purity, which became a popular holiday flower in the United States in the late 1800s.

The eating of ham on Easter Sunday is said to have survived from an old English bit of nastiness—showing contempt for the Jews by eating pork (a non-kosher food).

If it rains on Easter Sunday, it will rain for the next seven Sundays following.

If there was a white Christmas, then Easter will be green (and vice versa).

In the American Ozarks, people believe that an Easter morning bath taken before daybreak will help cure rheumatism.

EASTER EGGS

See also: CHARTS, Holidays
EASTER
RABBIT'S FOOT

Easter eggs come from a very early Germanic custom that honored the goddess Eastre, who was supposed to consider the hare or the rabbit sacred. It was believed that on Easter Eve the hare would lay eggs for all good children.

The egg is a universal symbol of life. It symbolizes the start of spring, the return of life to earth. Colored Easter eggs represent the return of the flowers to the land. A vestige of ancient fertility rites, Easter egg traditions also involve egg-rolling contests, a very old custom that we continue today. The last child to break his or her egg will have good luck during the year.

EENY, MEENY, MINY, MO

This popular children's rhyme (currently out of favor because of the racial slurs implicit in the modern version), actually comes from the ancient druid version (about the first century B.C.):

Eena, meena, mona, mite
Basca, lora, hora, bite,
Hugga, bucca, bau;
Eggs, butter, cheese, bread,
Stick, stock, stone dead—O-U-T!

It is thought by the theologian Charles Francis Potter (*Standard Dictionary of Folklore, Mythology and Legend*, 1949) that this chant, in one form or another, was an ancient magical rhyme used to choose human sacrifices for druidic ceremonies.

Today when we say eeny, meeny, miny, mo, it is a way of choosing up sides, or deciding who will be first to do a task.

ELEVENTH HOUR

The phrase at the eleventh hour means, of course, at the last minute. It comes from the Bible. The Book of Matthew says that all those hired at the eleventh hour were to be paid just as much as those laborers who had worked in the vineyards all day long.

ELVES

See SMALL FOLKS

EMERALDS

See also CHARTS, Birthstones

> *Who first beholds the light of day*
> *In Spring's sweet flowery month of May*
> *And wears an emerald all her life*
> *Shall be a loved and happy wife.*
> (Anonymous)

Since ancient times there have been legends about emeralds. The Romans believed the stones lost their brilliance in the presence of evil. The Peruvians worshipped an emerald as large as an ostrich egg. In India, they believed it was possible to learn the "knowledge of the soul of the Eternal" by giving emeralds to the gods as offerings. Almost everyone believed in the wonders performed by the emerald as an amulet. When an emerald is worn near the head, it is believed to provide protection from the evil eye (*See* EVIL EYE); when it is in a ring, it can detect poison. An emerald can also be worn as a symbol of victory by warriors after a battle.

The emerald is invaluable to people who do close work, because it is supposed to relieve eyestrain. It can blind snakes. It is the symbol of love, prosperity, kindness, and goodness. It is the stone of those born under the sign of Taurus.

The emerld has been known to keep people honest, to make them clever and funny, to improve their memories, and to make them excellent public speakers. The emerald also was a cure-all at ancient pharmacies.

ENGAGEMENT (ENGAGEMENT RINGS)

See WEDDING CUSTOMS

ETERNITY

The Chinese symbol for eternity combines rivers, and flowing water. The small splash mark at the top implies a higher meaning. It signifies that eternity is a higher order than life on earth has been.

Eternity

EVIL EYE

See also CROSS-EYED

The concept of the evil eye is probably the most powerful and the most pervasive superstition in the history of the world. "For every one that dies of natural causes, ninety-nine will die of the evil eye," says the ancient Jewish Talmud.

Imagine the terror of a primitive man when he looked into another's eyes and saw a reflection of his own image in those eyes. In ancient times, people believed that the eye was the window of the soul and that certain people had devillike powers to cause illness, death, or bad luck. Man reasoned, therefore, that if his reflection showed in another man's eyes it could only be for evil purposes. Since the ideas of evil and envy are very similar, it was believed that a person with the evil eye coveted your belongings and your good luck.

You've probably heard Jewish friends say, *kayn aynhorah*. It means (loosely translated from Yiddish), "May no evil eye harm you." It is always said after someone has bragged or called attention to a fortunate member of the family. It's a charm against the evil eye, and since it's been in constant use for over four thousand years, it must be considered pretty potent.

This kind of protection against the evil eye is especially necessary for children. The forces of the Devil are especially interested in beautiful, bright, talented children. Whenever someone praises a child, someone else must quickly say a *kayn aynhorah* for protection. The Chinese don't say *kayn aynhorah*. Their method is to say things in reverse: For example, if the child is especially pretty, they will insist that it is really an ugly child; or they will comment on the stupidity of a really intelligent child.

The Greeks count on their blue worry beads for protection, and the Arabs are very careful not to say *el ain* out loud. Today in the Mediterranean countries you can see a plastic blue eyeball suspended from car mirrors or on key chains as an amulet.

Besides charms and amulets, saliva is good protection; spitting over your left shoulder, for example, should be helpful. (*See* SALIVA) The ability to outstare the evil eye often works. In Egypt mascara (or kohl) drawn as a circle around the eye was believed to protect against the power of the evil eye.

There is some evidence that as long ago as prehistoric times, people believed in monsters with eyes of emeralds that could charm their enemies. In ancient Rome there were professional witches who were hired to bewitch enemies. This practice persisted and spread throughout Europe. By medieval times, the fear of the evil eye was so great that people were burned at the stake for possessing one.

How can you recognize the evil eye? Recognition factors vary greatly from region to region. In some places cross-eyes are a sign;

cowlicks or being left-handed is another way to tell; the ability to
tame animals scares a lot of people; and if you have different-colored
eyes than the average person in the area, you're suspect.

Hypnosis is the closest thing to the evil eye. Svengali was a perfect
example of a person who possessed the evil eye.

Honi soit qui mal y pense.
(Make sure the evil is not in the eye of the beholder.)

(motto of the
Order of the Garter 1349,
established by Edward III.)

EYE COLOR

Blue eyes are said to indicate intelligence and even divine powers (because blue is the color of Heaven). Gray eyes mean a person is
calculating. Green eyes indicate creativity.

Brown-eyed people like to flirt before marriage but are loyal
afterwards.

EYELASHES

See also BEARDS
        FINGERNAILS

The eyelash is a valuable talisman to wish upon; if one falls out,
put it on the back of your left hand, make a wish, place your right
hand (palm down) over the lash, and press. If the lash sticks to the
right palm your wish will come true.

There are silly people who blow away the lash after making a wish.
This is not a good idea, since eyelashes belong to that group of bodily
growths that are believed to be of great use to witches who want to
cast an evil spell on you. Remember, always save them.

EYE SHADOW

See also CIRCLES
EVIL EYE

Eye shadow was used in ancient Egypt to draw a circle around the eyes (as lipstick was used to draw a circle around the mouth) so that the evil eye couldn't enter through them. The Devil has no powers against the strength of a circle.

FAIRIES

See also SMALL FOLKS

Fairies are small, often invisible creatures. They can either be helpful or a nuisance; evil or whimsical; and they always live very close to human beings. They're everywhere, in almost every culture. They are almost always associated with the color green (*See* CHARTS, Colors) and sometimes with white.

There are two main types of fairies. One belongs to a nation of fairies who live in a group in fairyland, with a king and queen. The best part of fairyland is that there is no concept of time. Nobody ever grows old or dies.

The second sort of fairies are independent little creatures, who often attach themselves to a household. They check around carefully choose a house and family they want to live with, and then simply move in.

There is of course, a third type of fairies who aren't quite as invisible as some would like them to be. Some say they live in groups and cause trouble. But the latter assumption has never been proven.

Playwright James M. Barrie believed that every time a little child says, "I don't believe in fairies," an unhappy fairy dies just a little bit.

FATAL LOOK

At first glance (pardon the pun) the terms fatal look and evil eye may appear to be the same; but in the history of superstitions they're quite different. Fatal look, as in "if looks could kill," means a look that can literally kill someone instantly. The evil eye, on the other hand, is merely malevolent, causing bad luck or, at the worst, death over a prolonged period.

In Egyptian folklore, the story goes that Isis killed a spy with a single look when he was spotted watching her mourn the dead body of Osiris, her lover.

Throughout the centuries there have been people and creatures who were believed to have the power to kill with a glance. Some snakes, for instance, were believed to poison the air with their eyes.

FATHER TIME

The old man with long beard, scythe, and hourglass who turns up every New Year's Eve is the descendant of Saturn, who represented time. Father Time, as we know him, still carries the scythe to show he can destroy anything at will, and the hourglass is a sign of the unstoppable flow of years. The figure with the scythe has also frequently been pressed into service to represent death; hence the name of the Grim Reaper.

FEAR OF THE DARK

See also NIGHT AIR IS BAD FOR YOU

Having a fear of dark places isn't considered instinctive; it's a response to conditioning. Grandma used to say that night air was unhealthy because it would fill the house with poison. Grandma was only repeating an idea that *her* grandma had been taught: that air after sundown is harmful.

Long ago people thought that at night evil air rose from the ground and floated around, poisoning the atmosphere. Many sun worshippers hid until the sun came out because when it went away they felt they no longer had its protection.

Primitive man had every right to be afraid of the dark, since he lived in forests and caves where darkness often concealed wild animals. To help allay those fears, he created a god of darkness.

FERN SEED

Want to be invisible? Carry a fern seed in your pocket and the world won't be able to see you! Here's how it works: The fern seed is so tiny it was once thought not to exist at all. In early times it was believed to be invisible. Later, it was thought to exist only on Midsummer's Eve. If, on that night, you caught the seed in a white cloth before it touched the ground, you could gain its power of invisibility. (If you're interested in trying this, Midsummer's Eve is the night before summer begins.)

FIG SIGN

Try this: Make a fist, putting your thumb up between your index finger and your middle finger. You've just made a rude gesture that would make many Italians fighting mad!

In witchcraft, this gesture, known universally as the fig sign, is used against the evil eye. It can also be used when you've done something good and don't want the Devil to notice.

It's one of the more ancient finger gestures, and it is closely related to the more popular middle finger in the air that drivers the world over are so fond of using.

There's a legend that Barbarossa first used the sign to indicate contempt for the people of Milan after a battle.

FINGERNAILS

See also HAIR

Don't cut your fingernails on Friday or Sunday. Monday is a very good day to cut them, as this old English rhyme points out:

Cut nails on Monday you'll get good news,
Cut nails on Tuesday will bring new shoes,
Cut nails on Wednesday and you'll travel,
Cut nails on Thursday and you'll get more shoes,
Cut nails on Friday and there's money (or a toothache, or sorrow),
Cut them on Saturday and you'll see your lover on Sunday.
But cut them on Sunday and the Devil will get you.

(Anonymous)

In any case, it's a very chancy thing to cut your fingernails at all, because you never know who'll get hold of the parings and use them in a charm against you. Like other parts of the body, fingernails are believed to be parts of your soul that can be used by witches and other evil beings in potions and charms against you. (*See* BEARDS)

If you must cut your nails, and you've chosen the day of the week that's best for you, don't cut them in order—that invites death. (The nails on a corpse are usually cut in order.)

Dragon Lady nails, the very long kind the actress Gale Sondergaard made famous, were popular from ancient times right through to the nineteenth century in China, where they were considered a sign of great beauty and a symbol of distinction. They indicated that a person was an aristocrat and never worked with their hands. To protect the nails, these people wore sheaths of silver or gold on their fingertips.

There's another superstition, involving the white specks (calcium spots, probably) that many people have on their nails. The rhyme goes:

Specks on fingers,
Money lingers.
Specks on the thumb,
Money comes.

White specks on your fingernails indicate good fortune; on thumb-nails means you'll get a gift; on the forefinger, the number of friends; on the middle finger, the number of enemies; on the ring finger, a letter coming; and on the little finger, a journey.

Remember, the total number of white specks on your nails shows the world how many lies you've told!

FISH

See also TALISMAN

Better finish your fish—it's brain food. In the nineteenth century it was discovered that both fish and the human brain contain quite a lot of phosphorus, and since the concept of like makes like is ancient and still well received in many quarters, fish was considered brain food that would make you smart.

If you do eat fish, eat if from head to tail for good luck.

Some beliefs of fishermen are:

> If you count the number of fish you've caught, you won't catch any more that day.
>
> If the fish aren't biting, throw a fisherman into the water, then haul him out; the fish will come around then, probably out of curiosity.
>
> Throw the first fish caught back; in ancient times fishermen did this as payment to Poseidon (Neptune), the king of the sea.

In certain parts of the world the fish is sacred. In other parts, it is forbidden as food. In some parts of India it is said to be the food of ghosts.

To some people the fish is a symbol of fertility; in ancient Egypt it was believed to have eaten the phallus of the god Osiris. The Chinese consider it a sign of happiness and in most of India it is one of the eight symbols of Buddha and therefore sacred. Early Christians associated it with the Trinity, because Christ fed the multitudes with five loaves and two fishes.

FIVE
See also NUMBERS

To the Greeks, five was the symbol of the world. They believed that the five-pointed star represented the secrets of life.

There is a rumor that Pythagoras invented the five-pointed star as his symbol of geometric perfection. In the Middle Ages it became the wizard's star and was worn on cloaks as an emblem of the mysteries of the universe.

According to numerology the number five represents fire and love and marriage.

FLAGS MUST NEVER TOUCH THE GROUND

During a battle, a flag bearer always stayed near his king. The troops knew if he lowered the flag to the ground it meant the king was either dead or dangerously wounded. The superstition that it's bad luck for the flag to touch the ground comes from those early wars.

FLIP A COIN

Flipping a coin is an ancient way of deciding a point. People believed that when they flipped a coin, it was the gods who would be deciding the winner as the coin turned over and over in the air on its way to the ground. Later, Fate or Lady Luck made the decision.

The idea "heads you win, tails you lose" comes from Julius Caesar's day, when the emperor's head was on coins. If his head came up when you called it, the decision was made once and for all—Caesar always won.

FLOWERS CAUSE DEATH

Flowers in a hospital room were once thought to be unhealthy or fatal. This was a notion of the Victorians who believed that picked flowers decomposed to such a degree that they made the air unfit to breathe, causing illness and even death.

To illustrate this point the Victorians concocted a morality story, called "The Revenge of the Flowers," about two young girls who took a nap after picking flowers all afternoon. While they slept the spirits of the flowers asked why the girls had killed them and then breathed decomposing, noxious breaths into the sleeping girls' faces until the two were dead. The last line reads: "The flowers are avenged."

In the Language of Flowers, (See CHARTS) gathered flowers say, "we die together."

FLOWER LANGUAGE

See also CHARTS, Language of Flowers

> *Flowers are the sweetest thing that God ever*
> *made and forgot to put a soul into.*
> (Beecher, *Life Thoughts*, 1858)

As clever as "Say It With Flowers"—the slogan for the Society of American Florists—may be, it represents anything but a new or an original idea. Flowers have had secret meanings (and often mystical ones) attributed to them ever since Greek mythology. A language of flowers, one in which every flower expressed a special word or sentiment, was first popular in the Orient. It reached Europe during the early 1700s via Lady Mary Wortley Montagu, who went to Turkey with her husband and began sending back to England these first interpretations:

> *Clove—I have long loved you and you have not known it.*
> *Jonquil—Have pity on my passion.*
> *Pear Blossom—Give me some hope.*
> *Rose—May you be pleased, and your sorrow mine.*
> *Straw—Suffer me to be your slave.*
> *Cinnamon—My fortune is yours.*
> *Pepper—Send me an answer.*

The Language of Flowers gradually became very popular in England, and to some degree throughout the Continent, but it wasn't until Victorian times that it became all the rage. The intricacies of the game were overwhelming.

Explained by Claire Powell in *The Meaning of Flowers*, a flower, when presented upright, meant something good; when the flower was inverted, something bad. For example, a rosebud with thorns and leaves meant, "I fear you're never going to love me, but I still have hope." Returned upside down, it meant, "You must neither fear nor hope." If the rosebud was stripped of the thorns it meant, "There is everything to hope for"; stripped of its leaves, 'Your fears are correct." Inclined to the right, the flower implied a personal comment about the recipient; for instance, an inclined white lily said, "You are all purity and sweetness." Inclined to the left, the flower represented a personal message about the one who gave it.

This language gets more involved. If the flower was placed in the hair, it might mean caution; in the cleavage, rememberance or friendship; or over the heart, love. All of this depended upon the flower chosen. For example, if a marigold was placed in the hair, it expressed sorrow of mind; in the cleavage, boredom; and near the heart, pangs of love. It might well have taken an Oxford education to have understood what someone was trying to say with a simple daisy!

FORGET-ME-NOTS

> *sweet forget-me-nots,*
> *That grow for happy lovers*
> (Tennyson, *The Brook*)

Forget-me-nots have been a symbol of undying love since antiquity. They have also been used as tokens of friendship and remembrance.

Claire Powell, in her *Meaning of Flowers*, tells of an Austrian legend in which two lovers, on the eve of their wedding, walk along the banks of the Danube. A blue flower rides in on the waves, and the young bride sighs because she knows the flower will be swept away. Her lover jumps into the river to retrieve it, but a strong undertow drags him down. With his last effort he flings the flower onto the shore and drowning calls, "Love me. Forget me not!"

There's another, less romantic superstition that steel dipped into the boiling juice of the forget-me-not becomes hard enough to cut through stone. The juice is also said to cure both rabies and sore eyes.

The flower is traditionally given on February 29 as a symbol of remembering a day which only appears once every four years.

FORGETTING THINGS

There's a very popular superstition that if you've forgotten something it's bad luck to go back for it. The reason is that if you interrupt your journey by returning for the item, you'll have broken a circle (*See* CIRCLES), and that's very bad luck, indeed. There is help for this situation. Go back to where you left the forgotten object, sit down, make a wish or say a magic charm like this effective one:

If I sit, bad luck will flit

—and then count to ten.

Some people believe that women forget things more often than men. One African tribe, in its funeral procession for a dead woman, returns to the deceased's home for an hour so that the ghost can have a chance to collect the things she may have forgotten. (This saves the ghost a trip later.)

FOUR-LEAF CLOVER

One leaf is for hope, and one is for faith,
And one is for love, you know,
And God put another in for luck.
(Higginson, *Four-Leaf Clover)*

The druids were the first to believe in the power of the four-leaf clover. They were certain that possessing one allowed them to see evil spirits, like witches, which they could then avoid.

It was believed by some Christians that Eve took a four-leaf clover with her when she left the Garden of Eden.

The Irish say, "he's in clover," when someone is doing very well. Finding enough real, uncultivated four-leaf clovers to wear would be difficult, though—they are freaks of nature, a mutation of the common three-leaf variety.

FRIDAY

Alas! you know the cause too well;
The salt is spilt, to me it fell.
Then to contribute to my loss,
My knife and fork were laid across
On Friday, too! the day I dread;
Would I were safe at home, in bed!
(John Gay, *Fables*, Pt. I, 37, 1727)

Now Friday came. Your old wives say,
Of all the week's the unluckiest day.
(Anonymous)

It has often been pointed out that everything bad in history has happened on a Friday. Adam and Eve were supposed to have fallen from grace on Friday; the Flood started on a Friday; the Temple of Solomon fell on a Friday; and Christ was crucified on a Friday.

So, it's bad luck:
> to be born on a Friday
> to start a new job on a Friday
> to cut your nails on a Friday
> to visit the sick on a Friday
> to start a voyage on a Friday
> to change the bed linen on a Friday
> to open a new play on a Friday

Criminals say if you're sentenced on a Friday, you will receive a stiffer sentence. Friday was known as Hangman's Day because executions often took place on it.

Ships never set sail on Friday. That may be since H.M.S. Friday, a ship whose construction began on a Friday, set sail on a Friday, and was never heard from again!

Several major financial panics have contributed to the coining of the term Black Friday. The first happened on a Friday in England in December 1745, and was followed by a number of other similarly disastrous Fridays on the English stock market.

He who sings on Friday will weep on Sunday; then again, if it rains on Friday, it will be clear on Sunday.

FRIDAY THE THIRTEENTH

See also FRIDAY
        NUMBERS
        THIRTEEN
        THIRTEEN AT TABLE

Friday the Thirteenth is an especially unlucky day.

Twelve witches are necessary for a meeting—plus the Devil equals thirteen—and they always meet on Friday. The combination of Friday, a generally unlucky day, with thirteen, an especially unlucky number, can be terrifying.

FRINGE

See KNOTS

FROGS

See also WARTS

A favorite and powerful amulet of the Egyptians, Greeks, Turks, Italians, and others, the frog held an important place in early times. It was a symbol of inspiration and of fertility (due to the large number of eggs it lays at one time). The frog was so important in ancient Egypt that when one died, it was embalmed. It was a popular Roman mascot (*See* MASCOTS) and is still believed to be very good luck in the home. The first-century botanist Pliny the Elder believed a frog had powers that attracted friends and inspired lasting love in those who possessed one.

Others, however, believe that the frog holds the souls of dead children.

Even today the frog is still considered a fairly reliable weatherman because of its susceptibility to atmospheric changes, which cause it to croak whenever the barometers go down.

The ancients found the frog an inspiring creature and often carried amulets made in its image. Today we close our coats with frogs (ornamental cloth closings consisting of a button and a loop through which it passes), perhaps a holdover from an early French custom where frogs were embroidered onto clothes for good luck.

GAMBLING

Since almost all gambling is a matter of luck and good fortune, there are few if any explanations for the following superstitions:

   If you're having bad luck at cards, rise and turn three times with your chair in your hand—your luck will change.

   It's bad luck for any of the players, when a player places a matchstick across one that you've previously placed in the ashtray.

   It's bad luck for a woman to touch your shoulder while you're playing; it's also bad luck to meet a woman while on your way to the gambling room. (These are old superstitions, from times when most gamblers were men.)

No hand with the four of clubs is ever lucky. (The four of clubs is called the Devil's four-poster bed.)

Borrowed money can't lose.

Beginner's luck is indisputable.

It's bad luck to drop a card during the game.

If you sing while you play, your partner will lose.

If you are angry while playing, you'll lose.

He who borrows money to play will win; but he who lends money while playing will lose.

Rub dice on a red-headed person for luck.

Carry dice in a pocket all the time, and you'll have good luck.

If you find a die a certain way it means:

(one spot up) an important letter coming

(two spots) a long and good trip ahead

(three spots) a big surprise; sleep in a strange bed

(four spots) very unlucky—big trouble ahead

(five spots) unfaithfulness from your lover

(six spots) very lucky—you'll get money

Touch a hunchback for luck (*See* LUCK) (the gambler's word hunch comes from hunchback).

Always "back your luck"; in other words, stay with a lucky streak.

GARLIC

> *Garlick makes a man*
> *Winke, drinke, and stinke.*
> (Nashe, *Unfortunate Traveller*, 1594)

According to legend, a string of garlic bulbs worn to bed at night could protect you from vampires. As vampires became more and more infrequent night visitors, it was believed that the wreath of garlic bulbs in a house with illness could draw the disease away from the stricken person and absorb the illness.

Today many people tend to think that the garland of bulbs hung on the mantel will bring good luck.

Garlic cloves, we are told, can do wonderous things. They can stop bed-wetting, help toothaches, and when rubbed into the gums of a horse restore its failing appetite.

In classical Greece garlic was left as dinner for Hecate, the goddess of the dead. Since Hecate taught witchcraft and sorcery, garlic became closely associated with the world of the occult.

Certainly the strong aroma of garlic prolonged its life as a mystical substance. It is thought, for instance, that garlic is a good antiseptic —it isn't. In some places, the smell of garlic is believed to keep evil spirits away. Elsewhere it is believed to indicate the presence of evil.

Roman soldiers ate garlic to make them courageous. There are still South American bullfighters who take garlic cloves into the bullring with them, believing that the smell will stop the bull from charging. (It probably would stop a bull or an enemy from charging, if enough cloves were used!)

GARNETS

See Also CHARTS, Birthstones

> *By her who in this month was born [January]*
> *No gems save garnets should be worn;*
> *They will insure thee constancy,*
> *True friendship and fidelity.*
>
> (Anonymous)

Centuries ago Poles began wearing garnets as protection against illness. Later the stone became an amulet for world travelers. In Asia, garnets were used as an ancient form of bullet, and the Persians considered them the only stones good enough for royalty.

The Old Testament says that a large ruby-colored garnet was Noah's only source of light in the Ark during the Flood.

During the Middle Ages a garnet was especially important if it had a lion's head engraved on it. It was then thought to be blessed and to impart good health and honor to its wearers. This was a very rare amulet indeed, since garnets are hard and brittle and usually shatter during engraving.

GEMINI

See also TWINS
         ZODIAC

Gemini, a constellation first noted as early as 6000 B.C., is made up of the twin stars Castor and Pollux. It is the sign of those born between May 21 and June 20. Gemini, the Twins, has been associated throughout history with twins like the Roman rulers Romulus and Remus and the Chinese twin principles yin and yang. (*See* TWINS)

The sign of the Twins denotes a multifaceted personality, flexibility, and adaptability. Geminis are likable, impetuous, and good company to have around. They are clever, charming, and attractive. They are ruled by Mercury, which makes them fast and willing learners, but they tend to skim subjects rather than learn them. They are people of the air and changeable.

Gemini, the twins

Geminis also tend to be intelligent, but they procrastinate. They have strong nerves but get depressed by boredom, keep cool in a crisis, and should be involved in self-expressive pursuits.

Wednesdays are good for Geminis, the numbers three and four work well for them, and silver or gray are their good colors. Their birthstone is the agate.

Some famous Geminis are Judy Garland, John F. Kennedy, Marilyn Monroe, and Henry Kissinger.

GHOSTS

> *Ghosts do fear no laws*
> *Nor do they care for popular applause.*
> (Unknown, *Thomas Nash His Ghost*, 1600)

Either ghosts are human souls after death, or they don't exist at all. They might be products of an overactive imagination. They might also be people who have died a violent death or who have some unfinished business to do, who return to earth as ghosts to settle their affairs.

Whatever ghosts are, here's what you can do to protect yourself from them:

> Make a cross out of two pieces of fruitwood, tie it together with a piece of red string, and wear it between the lining and the fabric of your coat.

> When you meet a ghost, spit on the ground between you and the ghost and say, "In the name of the Lord, what do you wish?"

A ghost probably won't do you any harm, though, if you haven't harmed it during its lifetime.

> *From ghoulies and ghosties,*
> *Long-leggity beasties*
> *And things that go Bump in the night*
> *Good Lord deliver us.*
> (Scottish prayer, 1800)

GIFT HORSE IN THE MOUTH

We all know the famous Welsh proverb, "always look a gift horse in the mouth." Or is it "never look a gift horse in the mouth?" The second adage probably goes back to Homer, who said, "It is not good to refuse a gift." He may have been thinking of the tale about the Trojan horse—but to have looked that particular gift horse in the mouth would have been a very good idea.

Looking a horse in the mouth means counting its teeth to determine its age and, therefore, its value. Rabelais wrote: (*Works*, I, xi) "He always looked a given horse in the mouth," meaning you never get anything good for nothing, or something bought is often cheaper than a gift.

Perhaps the reverse is true. It's bad manners to look too carefully at a gift; it's an obvious attempt to determine how much it's worth.

Either look or don't look; but never turn your back on a gift horse (or a donkey).

GIVE A PIN, GIVE A PENNY

See PINS

GNOMES

See SMALL FOLKS

GOBLINS

See SMALL FOLKS

GOLDFISH

The first thing you need to know is that goldfish, those tiny, glittering things you win at the penny arcade, are members of the carp family and as such, have a long and happy tradition as a good luck talismans. The Egyptians kept them as mascots (*See* MASCOTS) and thought they were particularly helpful to lovers and insurance of peace and harmony within a household. The Greeks and Romans thought pretty much the same thing, extending the good luck to cover courting and marriage.

In the Orient, a yellow or gold carp was a mascot that brought good fortune as well as good luck to lovers. The goldfish is also an emblem of Buddha.

Claudia De Lys, in *A Treasury of American Superstitions*, tells about the Egyptians who believed that the carp had the perserverance to leap the great waterfall and to reach the chariot made of clouds, which would carry them to Heaven. Other fish didn't have the patience to persist, and simply drowned. That's probably why the carp became good-luck mascots.

GOOD FRIDAY

See also EASTER
         EASTER EGGS
         HOT CROSS BUNS

Good Friday is celebrated on the Friday before Easter. Like most of the other days of the Christian Holy Week, it became a holiday—for the day Christ died—in the fourth century. Prior to that, all the days of that week were treated as parts of the same celebration.

Some of the many superstitions connected with Good Friday are:

A loaf of bread or buns baked on Good Friday will not get moldy and will bring good luck for a year.

Bread baked on Good Friday and kept is a good luck talisman against shipwrecks.

Babies should be weaned on Good Friday.

The sun doesn't shine as brightly on Good Friday as it does on other days.

Breaking a dish on Good Friday is a good luck sign; it says that no damage will come to that house all year long.

Planting anything on Good Friday will produce a plentiful crop.

A ring blessed on Good Friday will bring protection for the year.

In Scandinavian countries, to insure against evil spirits, witches, and snakes, branches of mountain ash are placed around the door of homes. This will only work if done on Good Friday.

GOOD HEALTH

The Egyptians had a magical sign to bring them good health and to ward off illness and disease. This symbol was also believed to counteract the effects of the evil eye. The mere representation of an eye was used for protection. It might be painted on the prow of a ship to guard it against shipwreck or it might be painted on a cup or a plate to prevent breakage.

GOOD LUCK—GIVE OLD SHOES

See WEDDING CUSTOMS

GO TO THE DICKENS

This little euphemism has nothing to do with Charles Dickens and probably originated long before he was born. Shakespeare used it in the *Merry Wives of Windsor*: "I cannot tell what the dickens his name is."

According to the language expert Lewis B. Funk, dickens probably came from devilkins, meaning little devils. Today "go to the dickens" usually means "go to Hell."

GREMLINS

See SMALL FOLKS

GROOMS (BRIDEGROOMS)

See WEDDING CUSTOMS

GROUNDHOG DAY

If Candlemas Day be fair and bright,
Winter will have another flight.
But if Candlemas day brings clouds and rain,
Winter is gone and won't come back again.
                              (Old English proverb)

On February 2, it is said, the groundhog wakes up from its long winter snooze and pokes its head out from its underground hiding place. If it sees its shadow, there will be six more weeks of winter (if the sun is out, he will see his shadow and be frightened back to his nest). If there's no shadow, summer is on its way, and the groundhog will stay out and play. This modern superstition has more to do with harvesting and planting than with weather forecasting. Six more weeks of winter can't be very good for the farmer who would prefer a mild February.

This modern superstition has early origins. February 2 used to be Candlemas Day (and still is in some countries). Candlemas was the time when the candles were blessed for the year in observance of the Purification of the Virgin and the Presentation of Christ at the Temple.

An even earlier observance of this day was in Rome where it was the day to honor Venus.

GYPSIES

There are many theories about who gypsies really are. One legend says they are people condemned to wander the earth without rest because they refused hospitality to Joseph, Mary, and Jesus on their flight to Egypt. The word gypsy is a corruption of the word Egyptian. At least that was the medieval notion of the origin of the name gypsy.

The gypsies refer to themselves as Romany for many contradictory reasons that outsiders can't seem to fathom. They maintain an aura of mystery as a separate nation, it is thought, by following strict taboos against intermingling and revealing any of their secrets.

Some believe they migrated from Northern India in about 100 A.D. and proceeded to Central Europe by the 1400s. Others say they are descended from the outcasts of the temple of Thoth in Egypt.

Even today, the gypsy is characterized as a moon worshipper who is born, lives, and dies in the outdoors. They are fortune-tellers and horse handlers. They can read the tarot cards (*See* TAROT) and although they often believe in their own ability to see the future, they hardly ever give a real reading to an outsider. Gypsies believe that until a dead person has been burned, the soul roams the earth unable to get free of this world, remaining a constant accuser of those who have not burned the body.

HAIR

See also BEARDS
HAIR COLOR

Is your hair curly? Then you must be lucky! Since curly hair resembles the wavy rays of the sun, the sun god likes you and will protect you. You say your hair got curly by eating bread crusts; but have you heard about pouring rum or grapes on your head in order to make your hair grow curly?

Down in the southern states they say that combing your hair at night makes you forgetful.

Since ancient Egyptian times people have believed that hair clippings can be used by a witch in casting evil spells. The Egyptians believed that a potion made of hair, nail clippings, and human blood could produce absolute power over another person.

A hairy chest has always been a sign of strength; and cut hair has been, since Samson and Delilah, a sign of weakness. There's a myth that hair changes color overnight; and that hair and fingernails continue to grow after death, they don't; and be careful—whistling causes your beard to grow.

HAIR COLOR

There was never a saint with red hair.
(Old Russian proverb)

If you pull out a gray hair, seven will come to its funeral.
(Old Pennsylvania proverb)

Gray hair is a sign of age, not wisdom.
(Old Greek proverb)

A chaste woman ought not to dye her hair yellow!
(Menander, 310 B.C.)

Trust no man
Even your own brother
Whose hair is one color
And beard is another.
(Anonymous)

Blondes are fickle and make false friends. Brunettes are sincere and have good health. Redheads are emotionally unstable and have terrible tempers.

Redheads really come in for criticism. Since red is the color of fire, Romans, Egyptians, and Greeks all thought that redheads were particularly unlucky people to have around. In the Middle Ages, it was believed that redheads were witches and therefore deserved to be burned.

Some superstitions about hair color are:
It's good luck to run your hand through the hair of a redhead.
It's lucky if a dark-haired person crosses the threshold first on New Year's Day.
Bees always sting redheads.

Redheads are good conversationalists.

Curly black hair means neatness; straight black hair, extravagance; and thick black hair, good health.

Brunettes have the best chance of survival except when disease strikes—then blondes fare better.

Men with dark hair are deceitful.

HALLOWE'EN

See also CHESTNUT

October 31 was, according to the Celtic calendar, the last day of the year and a time to honor the dead. The druids celebrated that day by inviting the souls of all the evil people who, upon death, were sentenced to live in the bodies of animals to a feast to see if their deeds since death earned them redemption. On that night, ghosts and witches walked the earth; some said they journeyed for two days. You can imagine what sort of havoc was created and why it was unsafe for decent folk to be out on that terrifying night. It was called All Evil Day, or something similar.

In 837, Pope Gregory IV changed the name to All Saints Day and discouraged the common belief that witches and evil spirits went partying. The word hallow was an old English one meaning saint or holy man, in common usage until the fifteenth century. All Hallow Eve became All Souls Eve or All Saints Eve. Hallowe'en is simply a contraction of the original. (In Italy and other places it is still All Saints Eve.)

Symbols and superstitions of the day are:

Ghosts and hobgoblins roam the earth, but since they are invisible, children dressed as adults perform their mischievous pranks for them.

Black cats (*See* BLACK CAT) are Satan in disguise and can be seen cavorting with witches.

Pumpkins, a symbol of harvesttime, are cut to resemble faces, and a candle lighted inside the pumpkin pays tribute to the sun at harvesttime.

The disagreeable custom of chalking a person's back comes from

merry old England, where they drew white circles on backs
to indicate that summer was over and the rule of the sun was
coming to an end for another year. (*See* CIRCLES)
Fortune-telling is very popular on this night and started when
witches got together to feast during druid times and told
each others' futures.

HANDS

See also PALMISTRY

The old German proverb that says "Warm hands, cold heart" or
"cold hands, loving spirit" (whichever seems appropriate) is little
more than a compliment for people with cold hands.

If your right palm itches you'll get money, but if your left palm
itches you'll have to pay money out.

Don't wash a baby's hand, or you'll wash away its luck.

HANDSHAKE

Two things happen when you shake hands: You make a cross with
your clasped palms; and you effectively put your weapon hand
(unless you're left-handed) out of commission, so it can do no harm.

Handshaking is not a worldwide custom. In the Orient, for instance, people, in meeting, have joined their own hands in front of
them for centuries; they are effectively proving their good intentions
by placing their hands where they can be seen, away from their
weapons.

Do you think muggers could be taught this simple little gesture?

HAT ON BED, HAT ON TABLE

A hat on a bed is bad luck and will cause a fight in a household.

In the Orient it was believed that placing a hat (or turban) where another person might lay his or her own head was a dangerous business. This was a way one might contract bad luck from the evil eye. (*See* EVIL EYE)

Long ago people believed that evil spirits lived in the hair. They based this idea upon the crackling sound they sometimes heard, which is caused by static electricity.

The superstition about putting a hat on a table is like the superstition about putting your hat on a bed. Putting your hat on a table, however, will let evil spirits get into your food.

HATS

For good luck, turn your hat front to back; it's symbolic of changing the natural order of things and is supposed to be quite helpful in warding off bad luck. Jockeys do it, as do ball players sometimes.

Remember, wearing a hat indoors causes a headache.

HELL

> *The descent to hell is easy; the gates*
> *stand open night and day; but to reclimb*
> *the slope, and escape to the upper air,*
> *this is labor.*
>
> (Virgil, *Aeneid*, VI)

Hell appears to be what bores or frightens each person the most. It is also known as Hades or any one of an endless string of euphemisms—even New York is called a helluva town.

Hell is the opposite of Paradise. It is where mortal souls go because of bad behavior during life. Hell is also God's way of condemning a mortal for lack of faith.

In the world of superstition, Hell is the place where the Devil and his playmates come from, it is where the evil eye resides, and it is the most frightening place a superstitious person can imagine. At the mention of Hell such a person will spit three times, turn around seven times, knock on wood, touch iron, or perform any other counstercharm that might help avoid a meeting with the Devil, and going to Hell.

HEXES AND HEX SYMBOLS

The Pennsylvania Dutch are fond of putting gaily painted symbols on their barns to frighten away the Devil and to protect their animals from the evil eye. The symbols usually contain a good deal of red, a color that frightens witches. The word hex does not come from hexagon, although hex symbols are frequently six-sided.

Hexes are spells, the stuff of which witchcraft is made. A witch, or more often a warlock, will place a hex on a person or thing to cause trouble. Even today there are professional hex doctors, who make a hex to order. There are spells for all the evils that can befall people. (It can be a very lucrative business.) The spells come mostly from medieval times and are contained in two very important handbooks, *Seventh Book of Moses* and *The Long Hidden Friend*.

HICCUPING

Sneezing will stop a hiccup.
(Hippocrates, 400 B.C.)

Aristophanes suggested holding your breath or gargling with water as a cure for it. Later, more sophisticated people suggested remedies like spitting on the forefinger of the right hand, crossing the front of the left shoe three times, and repeating the Lord's Prayer backward.

Hiccups were said to have been caused by the evil eye. (*See* EVIL EYE) When they happened in Church, it was an indication that a person was possessed by the Devil.

If you can say the Lord's Prayer backward on one breath and then repeat three times:

> *Lick up, hiccup*
> *Stick up, hiccup*
> *Trick up, hiccup*
> *Begone, hiccup*

—you will be cured.

Scaring someone out of their hiccups works, generally, because it breaks the tension that may have caused them in the first place. (You might also believe that scaring the person often scares the evil spirits away.)

To stop hiccuping, you can:

hold your nose, tilt your head back, and take a sip of water for each year of your age

drink a glass of water from the far edge of the glass or through a napkin

bring your little fingers as close together as you can without having them touch

hold your breath and say hiccup nine times

If none of the above work, start over again from the top.

HOBSON'S CHOICE

Hobson's choice isn't a superstition. At the end of the sixteenth century Thomas Hobson owned a livery stable in Cambridge, England. Each customer who came to rent a horse had to take the animal nearest the door; there was no picking or choosing. Hobson's choice, of course, was no choice at all. Hobson is reputed to have explained that his policy was to have every customer alike well served, and every horse ridden with the same justice.

A common expression goes, "where to elect there is but one, 'tis Hobson's choice—that or none."

HOCUS-POCUS

Hocus-pocus may have started with a Norse sorcerer named Ochus, Bochus. It may also be a shorter version of hokuspokus-filiokus, which was a popular sacrilegious mockery of part of the Catholic mass, *hoc est corpus filii* ("this is the body of the Son"). It certainly has a important place in the history of witchcraft.

Thomas Ady's *A Candle in the Dark; or A Treatise Concerning the Nature of Witches and Witchcraft* (written in 1656) contains an early description of hocus-pocus:

> *I will speake of one man . . . that went about in King James' time . . . who called himself 'The Kings Majesties most excellent Hocus Pocus', and so he was called, because that at the playing of every Tricke, he used to say, 'Hocus pocus, tonus talontus, vade celeriter jubeo,' a dark composure of words, to blinde the eyes of the beholders, to make his trick pass the more currantly without discovery.*

Early in the seventeenth century, magicians, conjurers, and jugglers went by the name Hocus Pocus or variations of it, as they traveled around the countryside practicing their trade.

Today, hocus-pocus simply means flimflam, nonsense, or charlatanism.

The word hoax is a shortened version of hocus-pocus.

HOLLY

Before Christ, holly was loved in Rome. It was an emblem of friendliness and goodwill and was sent to friends as gifts during midwinter celebrations.

In Northern Europe people hung holly at their doors so that wood spirits could shelter themselves against the chilly winds in it, and to insure good luck.

Holly became a Christmas symbol almost immediately after the death of Christ. Some people believed that the Cross was of holly wood, which was punished by being turned into a scrub. Others say that Christ's crown of thorns was made of holly and that the berries had been yellow, until the crucifixion, when they turned red from his blood.

Two superstitions are that bringing holly into the house before Christmas Eve will provoke family quarrels and that holly must be burned after the twelve days of the holiday.

Witches hate holly. That's why some people grow it around their windows.

Holly is supposed to repel lightning, and the syrup from its bark, to cure coughs.

HONEYMOONS

See also WEDDING CUSTOMS

> *When a couple are newly married, the first*
> *month is honeymoon, or smick-smack.*
> (John Ray, *English Proverbs*, 1670)

It was once customary for a newlywed couple to drink a potion containing honey (usually mead mixed with honey) on each of the first thirty days of their marriage. During such a period the moon goes through all of its phases and then disappears. The affection of newlyweds was therefore regarded as waning like the moon. Hence the term honeymoon, a combination of the honey potion and the phases of the moon.

It has been reported that Attila the Hun drank so much of this honey and mead concoction that he suffocated to death during his honeymoon.

"The first month after marriage . . . there is nothing but tenderness and pleasure," said Samuel Johnson (in *Boswell: A Life*, 1755). That might well have been what the early bridegroom had in mind when he stole his bride and hid out for a month to escape the wrath of his new in-laws. In merry Old England, the most common way for a man to get married was for him to simply steal his bride, something he learned from his predecessor, the cave man. Some say that's how the honeymoon period got started, with the name and the pleasure coming later.

> *The honeymoon is the period during which the bride trusts the bridegroom's word of honor.*
>
> (Anonymous)

HORSESHOES

See also IRON

There are dozens of reasons why the horseshoe is lucky. First of all, there's the shape. Since the earliest of recorded times, man has believed that the crescent or u-shape was the most powerful protective sign. We see this in the arched windows of old churches, temples, and mosques (as well as in the arched doorways of modern churches and public buildings). These were built in that shape as a protection against evil.

Second, the horseshoes are nailed with seven iron nails. (*See* IRON, SEVEN) Seven is probably the most important number in the world of superstition. The nails used by blacksmiths have magic as powerful as the horseshoe itself. Rings made from these nails are said to give the same protection against evil as the horseshoe.

When you put a found—it's important that you find it—horseshoe over the doorway, or on the front of a barn as an amulet, you are following in the footsteps of the Greeks and the Romans who believed firmly in the protective powers of the horseshoe. Some say that if you hang the horseshoe with the prongs up, should the Devil get too close he will be sucked in and destroyed. Others say that if you hang it with the prongs down, the magic pours out and prevents the Devil from coming in at all. Whichever way you hang it, the important thing is that it's hung securely or its magic won't bring good luck; instead it will send you straight to the hospital.

There's a legend about Saint Dunstan, a blacksmith in England who later became the Archbishop of Canterbury. He was asked by a figure in a cloak to shoe him instead of his horse. Remembering that Satan had cloven hooves, which needed shoes, Dunstan nailed Satan to the wall and poked him with a red-hot poker until Satan agreed never to enter a house with an inverted horseshoe protecting its door.

HOT CROSS BUNS

Crosses made on food, either with a knife or icing, were thought to keep evil spirits away from the house. These foods became especially popular during holidays, when evil spirits liked to cause problems for the celebrants.

There is a superstition that hot cross buns baked on Good Friday will stay fresh for a year; and as long as they remain fresh, the men of the house who are sailors will not drown. (They may, however, get very bad cramps from these old buns.) (*See* EASTER)

> *One a penny, two a penny,*
> *Hot cross buns,*
> *If you have no daughters,*
> *Give them to your sons;*
> *If you have none of these*
> *   merry little elves*
> *Then you may keep them all*
> *   for yourselves.*
> (The street vendor's cry)

IF LOOKS COULD KILL

See EVIL EYE
      FATAL LOOK

ILL WIND

Over four hundred years ago John Heywood wrote (in *Proverbs*, II:VII) "It's an ill wind that bloweth no man to good." Shakespeare wrote, "Ill blows the wind that profits nobody." (*Henry IV*, II:V)

The Old Norse language meaning of the word ill was evil, and that's the meaning implied in the phrases about an ill wind.

The idea that someone profits from every disaster has followed us through the centuries. Some modern lyricists have often used the expression.

INSIDE OUT

See CLOTHING

IRIS

> *For wheresoev'er thou art in this world's globe,*
> *I'll have an Iris that shall find thee out.*
> (Shakespeare, *Henry VI, III:2*)

Iris was the goddess of the rainbow, and her name has been applied to the flower because of the many colors in which it blooms. Legend has it that Iris was the bearer of news from Zeus, who hardly ever left Mount Olympus.

In the Victorian Language of Flowers, an iris meant, "My compliments, I have a message for you."

IRON

See also HORSESHOES

Imagine how surprised primitive man must have been when he discovered iron. It could break wood and stone and withstand fire. It must certainly have been a gift from the gods, if a frightening one. To make iron, ancient man cut pieces of meteorites which were believed to have come from Heaven.

Long ago people believed that if iron touched a plant that was used for healing purposes, the plant would lose its powers. Iron was used for healing, though. A piece of iron was nailed to a tree after having been applied to the part of the body where the illness was. Their belief was that the illness would be trapped in the tree.

If you nail an iron amulet to the outside of your house, it will protect you from witches. Witches are terrified of iron. They have no powers against it at all, since iron is a special gift of the gods.

ITCHING

See also HANDS

What causes an itch? People in ancient times couldn't explain it except to consider it a craving. Thus the following sayings were born:

About an itching ear—Left for might,
                     Right for spite.

                     Left or right,
                     Good at night.

About an itching nose—If your nose itches.
                              Your mouth is in danger—
                              You'll kiss a fool,
                              And meet a stranger.

                              If your nose itches,
                              If your nose itches,
                              A stranger is coming
                              With a hole in his britches.

About an itching eye—If your left eye itches it's
                              itching for bad;
                              If your right eye itches good luck
                              is coming.

About an itching palm—You'll receive money from an
                              unknown source.

                    You'll take a bride.

In either case, as Shakespeare pointed out in *Julius Caesar*, it's not a good trait:

> *Let me tell you, Cassius, you yourself*
> *Are much condemned to have an itching palm.*

IVY

Ivy was popular in Victorian times. It represented friendship and fidelity. The Victorians often wore brooches that showed ivy growing around a fallen tree, with the inscription "Nothing can detach me from it."

The plant was sacred to the Egyptians, and the Greeks always used it to make victory crowns for their conquering armies.

Like most plants, ivy has been considered useful as a cure for all sorts of afflictions, especially sunburns, wounds, and swelling.

JADE

Much of the jade deposits of the world are found in China, and so it's not surprising that the Chinese have always worn jade as an amulet. It is thought to protect against stomachaches, to bring rain, and to help make men fertile.

In China, a piece of jade placed in the mouth or on the eyelids of a deceased person was believed to help bring back the spirit for another life on earth.

JINX

See also CHARMS

Many of us believe that people or things can be jinxed. Most of us use the word and believe in the idea that a continual run of bad luck is a jinx. It doesn't effect us much, though, unless we're gamblers, actors, accident-prone people, or sailors. Certain ships and theaters are said to be jinxed. (*See* FRIDAY, THEATRICAL FEARS)

There's little a person can do about a jinx, except to ride it out and be careful.

JUNE WEDDINGS

See WEDDING CUSTOMS

JUNIPER BERRIES

Today many people think that juniper berries help ward off bad vibrations when mixed in a potion called gin. The more we drink of this potent magic, the better the protection.

The Greeks appeased the gods of the underworld by burning the berries and the branches as incense. They also burned the berries at funerals to ward off evil spirits.

Today juniper berries often provide the perfume used in air purifiers. Some people also think that the perfume from the berries is a good luck charm against evil.

In the Victorian Lanugage of Flowers the juniper berry, given as a gift, meant protection and asylum from enemies.

KAYN AYNHORAH

See EVIL EYE

KEEP YOUR FINGERS CROSSED

See CROSS YOUR FINGERS

KISSING

> *Lord! I wonder what fool it was that*
> *first invented kissing.*
> (Jonathan Swift, *Polite Conversation*, 1738)

There's a story that the fool who first invented kissing did it as a way to see if his wife had been drinking wine behind his back. It is said that the Romans also used to press their lips on their wives' to test for sobriety.

Later the kiss was used to sign the deal after a marriage contract had been arrived at; hence the betrothal kiss. (*See* WEDDING CUSTOMS)

Kissing is thought to have started in Asia Minor as an expression of loyalty, and of sentiment—a mother kissing her child.

KNIFE AND FORK

There are many superstitions attached to knives, probably because originally a knife was a very personal possession, used by the owner to do everything from cutting up food to fighting and hunting.

It was believed that knives could serve as protection against evil spirits. A knife stuck into a door would protect a house from unlucky influences, while sticking a knife into the head of a cradle would protect the baby from bad luck. In Scotland, the sudden gusts of wind which appear on a calm day were supposed to be caused by the passing of invisible witches or fairies. Bad luck could be averted by throwing a knife across the whirling dust thrown up by their passage.

Crossed knives and forks on a table after a meal mean that a quarrel will follow. There is a long-standing fear of crossing dangerous objects, dating back to the time when crucifixion was used as a method of punishment, and emphasized by the fact that Jesus was crucified on a cross.

A dropped knife means good luck. If a knife falls and the blade sticks in the ground it means that a visitor is coming – in England it will be a man, in America a woman. If a dropped knife does not stick in the ground, there will probably be a fight.

In some regions, it is believed to be unlucky to sharpen a knife after sunset – this is inviting a burglar or enemy to enter the house during the night. If you live on a farm, and happen to leave a knife on a table overnight, it means that one of the farm animals will have died by day-break, and the knife will be needed to flay it.

The most common superstition attached to knives is that, because they are sharp-cutting, they will sever a friendship if they are given as a present. To prevent this, the knife must be symbolically bought by giving something in exchange, such as a penny. Some say that when the penny has been given, the following rhyme must be said:

> "If you love me, as I love you
> No knife can cut our love in two."

The friendship will then be safe.

KNOTS

To catch an evil spirit, and stop it from causing trouble, make a knot. Evil spirits are known to get caught at the spot where a knot is tied. The best example of this widespread belief is the clerical collar. It was feared that evil spirits would be caught in the priest's tie if it were knotted and hide there and cause trouble during religious ceremonies.

Some people tie knots on their kitchen aprons for protection, and some tie pieces of red string around a wart as a cure.

In medieval times if a knot was tied during a wedding it meant that the couple would never have children. This was considered such strong magic that the only way to break the spell was to untie the knot. Today, in many parts of the world, all knots in a house are untied during childbirth to make the delivery easier and safer.

The knot remains of paramount importance in wedding ceremonies. It symbolizes love and duty and an indestructible relationship. It is often represented by knots in the bridal bouquet. (*See* WEDDING CUSTOMS) In India, all knots in the clothing of the bridal party are loosened before a marriage, and retied at the wedding ceremony as a symbol of eternal unity.

Knotted fringe has a special place in religious ceremonies. The fringe keeps evil away by entangling the spirits, and when the fringe is knotted, it adds an extra layer of protection by confusing the spirits and then trapping them in the knots. Orthodox Jews add an extra bit of protection from any spirits that might get trapped by knotting the fringe in such a way as to spell out one of the sacred, unspoken names of God.

LADDERS

See WALKING UNDER LADDERS

LADYBUG, LADYBUG

Ladybug, ladybug, to your home you must turn,
Your house is on fire and your children may burn.
                    (Early English nursery rhyme)

Never, never kill a ladybug; it will inevitably bring bad luck.

If a ladybug lands on you when you are ill, she will take the illness away with her.

   The ladybug, a member of the beetle family, came to earth via lightning, according to an ancient Norse belief. It was closely associated with the goddess of love and beauty.
   There appears to be an uncanny empathy between children and ladybugs. Children tend to talk to them and expect an answer.

LAST SUPPER, THE

See THIRTEEN AT TABLE

LEFT-HANDED

See also RIGHT SIDE OF THE BED

   Left-handed people have always been discriminated against, since a left-handed person was thought to be a messenger of the Devil. It's common knowledge that the Devil lives on the left side of the body. In most modern languages terms like left-handed mean indirection, insincerity, and even treachery.
   Although about seven percent of the population is born left-handed, as children many are taught to be right-handed. It is believed that if left-handed people are made to use their right hands, they will stutter.
   Left-handed people are supposed to be clumsy. The Book of Judges, however, says: "There were seven hundred chosen men left-handed; everyone could sling stones at a hair breadth, and not

miss." Leonardo da Vinci painted the *Mona Lisa* with his left hand.

The Moslems have always been very concerned about left-handed people. They say that each Moslem has two guardian angels on earth; the one who lives on the right side takes note of all his or her good deeds; while the one on the left notes all the bad things. They also believe that at the Creation, God threw one fistful of dust to the right, creating people who would be happy, and one fistful of dust to the left, creating people who would be unhappy. The Moslems reserve the use of the left hand for all unclean acts: for example, petting dogs, which are unclean to Moslems.

In the Middle Ages, being left-handed was a sure sign of witchcraft and a reason to be burned at the stake.

LEO

See also ZODIAC

Leo, the Lion, is the astrological sign for those born between July 23 and August 22. Ruled by the sun, Leo is also a fire sign, which gives people born under it enthusiasm. There is an Egyptian legend that tells of Leo as the symbol for the heat of summer, the time when the Nile was said to overflow and lions to appear.

Leos tend to be generous, gracious, gregarious, and courageous. They like to do things their own way. Sometimes they are egotists, and they may marry for money instead of love.

Leos have active imaginations and can easily please an audience. They give orders easily and are impulsive leaders who try to rule. They are most effective in a crisis.

Sunday is a good day for Leos; five and nine are good numbers for them; and golden tones are their best colors. The birthstone for Leo is the sardonyx.

Some well-known Leos are Mae West, Alex Haley, Jacqueline Kennedy Onassis, George Meany, Benito Mussolini, Cecil B. De Mille, and George Bernard Shaw.

 Leo the Lion

LEPRECHAUNS

See SMALL FOLKS

LET GEORGE DO IT

This peculiar expression was first credited to King Louis XII of France who, in a sarcastic moment, said it about his minister Georges d'Amboise (later Archbishop of Rouen) who was a true Renaissance man and excelled in many areas. In fact, Louis was hard put to find something that George couldn't do. An expanded version, "Let George do it; he's the man of the Age," was quite popular among the people of France in the late fifteenth century.

The expression popped up in America when the cartoonist George McManus called his comic strip "Let George Do It."

There's also a saying that no man named George has ever been hanged (the accuracy of which I could not guarantee).

LIBRA

See also ZODIAC

Libra is the sign of the balance, or justice. It implies a strong love of justice and an eternal search for balance. This is the sign for those born between September 23 and October 22.

Libras are ruled by Venus, which makes them unusually artistic and creative, as well as sensitive. Their overriding concern in life is beauty and art. They love beauty in all forms. They are independent, intolerant, and idealistic; they often complain. They also search for justice and follow intellectual pursuits. Libras are under the influence of the air sign and are changeable, though clearheaded and quick to act once they make a decision. They are easily disturbed emotionally, and they need incentives to succeed.

Libra, the scales

Fridays are good days for Libras, and the numbers six and nine are usually lucky for them. Blue is their color. Libras are beautiful people, often charming and amusing, and always survivors. Their birthstone is the opal. They often have back problems.

Some famous Libras include David Ben-Gurion, Truman Capote, Carole Lombard, Dwight Eisenhower, Sarah Bernhardt, and Barbara Walters.

LIGHTING THREE CIGARETTES ON A MATCH

See THREE ON A MATCH

LIGHTNING

What did you hear? that God was bowling and the thunder was the sound of the pins falling and the lightning was a strike? did you hear the one about God being angry? If you heard the second explanation, that's the one that ancient civilizations believed. They were terrified by lightning and would fall on their faces in the dirt, believing that evil spirits were in the air all around them. They thought that lightning must be either a god (Thor, Jupiter, Zeus) or that it came from a god. When fires were started by lightning, they thought it a punishment from Heaven and wouldn't allow it to be extinguished.

There is a Hindu saying that goes, "Lightning strikes the loftiest tree first;" that makes sense. But the saying, "lightning never strikes the same place twice," isn't even logical. It's true that the law of averages is against it striking twice, but since lightning strikes an exposed area or structure, it can and has hit the same spot several times.

Some superstitions about lightning are that: A dog's tail draws lightning to it—don't believe it; acorns are supposed to be good protection against lightning when placed near windows (*See* ACORN); holly used at Christmastime is good protection (*See* HOLLY); and lightning turns milk sour unless a rusty nail has been added.

Weather watchers say:

> Forked lightning at night
> The next day clear and bright.

An Old English rhyme goes:

> Beware of an oak:
> It draws the strokes;
> Avoid an ash:
> It counts the flash;
> Creep under the thorn:
> It can save you from harm.

LILY OF THE VALLEY

Were lilies of the valley created by Eve's tears as she was expelled from the Garden of Eden; or are they, as the Irish say, fairy ladders that the small folks (See SMALL FOLKS) run up and down on, ringing the bells?

One legend says that Saint Leonard, a young Christian, went out to fight a dragon (which was really evil in disguise). Saint Leonard won, but he was wounded. As his blood fell to the ground the fragile little lilies grew to commemorate the battle Saint Leonard won for Christ (and the forces of good).

The lily of the valley stands for purity and humility. In early Christian times, it was dedicated to the Virgin Mary. In fact, in Great Britain and in France it is also known as "Our Lady's Tears."

The flower is believed to be able to cheer up a sad person; to help with a weak memory; and to stop the pain of gout.

Today the flower is still popular in bridal bouquets and actually is used in some medical treatments for heart disease.

It is the flower for those born in the month of May, and means the return of happiness.

LIPSTICK

See CIRCLES

LITTLE BIRD TOLD ME, A ·

See BIRDS

LOVE APPLE

See TOMATO

LOVE AT FIRST SIGHT

> *She lovede right fro the firste sighte.*
> (Chaucer, *Troilus and Criseyde* II, 1375)

> *Loving comes by looking.*
> (Latin proverb)

> *Whoever loved that loved not at first sight?*
> (Marlowe & Chapman, *Hero and Learning* I, 1598)

To the Greeks, it was common knowledge that each of us was part of someone else; we had been divided at birth, and the search for a mate was a search for the other half. When the two natural halves met they would know each other. This would be love at first sight.

The little purple flower known as love-in-idleness is said to have been pierced by Cupid's arrow and then reclaimed by the fairies. It is the flower most closely associated with love at first sight; as Shakespeare observed in *A Midsummer Night's Dream* (II:1):

> *Yet mark'd I where the bolt of Cupid fell:*
> *It fell upon a little Western flower,*
> *Before milk-white, now purple with love's wound,*
> *And maidens call it love-in-idleness.*
> *Fetch me that flower; The herb I shew'd thee once:*
> *The juice of it on sleeping eyelids laid*
> *Will make or man or woman wildly dote*
> *Upon the next live creature that it sees.*

LOVE-IN-IDLENESS

See LOVE AT FIRST SIGHT

LUCK

See also THEATRICAL FEARS

All the world of superstition is based upon luck—good luck and its sinister twin, bad luck.

"Luck is a mighty queer thing," wrote Bret Harte in *The Luck of Roaring Camp*. "All you know about it for certain is that it's bound to change." Luck is something that's always around. It can't be willed, bought, or bribed, although the ancients spent most of their waking hours trying to do just that. When they spoke of evil spirits, they meant bad luck. It was their way of explaining why things went wrong.

A senior Rothschild once advised:
> *Never have anything to do with an unlucky place or an unlucky man. I have seen many clever men, very clever men, who had not shoes on their feet. I never act with them. Their advice sounds very well, but they cannot get on themselves; and if they cannot do good to themselves, how can they do good to me?*

A momentary spate of bad luck is often cured by:
   holding your right hand to your face and spitting three times through your forefinger and middle finger
   making the fig sign (*See* FIG SIGN)
   pulling out your pockets and turning around in a circle (clockwise) three times (*See* CIRCLES)

Beginner's luck is usually good luck because there is some good magic in anything new.

A lucky man is rarer than a white cow.
(Juvenal, *Satires* VII)

It is a very bad thing to become
accustomed to good luck.
(Publilius Syrus, first century B.C.)

LUCKY AT CARDS, UNLUCKY IN LOVE

This proverb simply means you can't have everything. It probably dates to the Italians, who often shrugged about bad luck. They would say: He who is lucky in love should never play cards.

LUCKY BREAK

See also WISHBONES

Lucky break is a poolroom term referring to one or more balls going into pockets during the player's first turn. Circus people use the reverse; they say, "it broke bad," if the weather is bad, causing business to be off and bringing bad luck.

All this goes back to primitive times when a tribal member would break a stick in the middle to make a noise that would frighten away evil spirits. If things went well it was a lucky break.

A vestige of that is snapping your fingers at the mention of trouble to scare away bad thoughts or evil spirits.

MAKE A WISH
See BANANA
  MOON
  ROBIN REDBREAST
  STARS
  WISH ON A STAR

MANDRAKE ROOT

The reputed powers of the mandrake root came from the magical shape of the root when it is pulled out of the earth. This is one of the few natural objects that has the shape of the human body. It looks, in fact, as though it has been carved to order. The root so strongly resembles a man (or woman) with his legs spread that it has had sexual connotations since early Greek times. The Emperor Julian is said to have drunk a solution of mandrake root soaked in wine each night as an aphrodisiac before going to bed. Today, in some sections of Greece, young men carry a piece of the root in their pockets as a love charm. John Donne, referring to the root's attributes as a fertility drug, (in *Go and Catch a Falling Star*) wrote, "Get with child a mandrake root." (*See* APHRODISIACS)

Given the shape of the root, it isn't surprising that the ancients, who believed strongly in the concept of like makes like, believed that the root had the power to make a woman pregnant. It is also not surprising that, because of its shape, it would take on frightening and mystical powers. The Greeks believed in its powers for relieving pain. It was supposed to scare away the Devil. During the Middle Ages it was used as an anesthetic. In Arabia it was called the devil's candle because it was supposed to shine in the dark.

These roots were believed to grow under the gallows of murderers, nourished by the body's drippings. When these roots were torn up from the ground, they were said to utter piercing shrieks that brought death to those who heard them.

The mandrake root is mentioned in the Bible; Thomas Newton (18th century) in his *Herball to the Bible*, wrote, "It is supposed to be a creature having life, engendered under the earth, of the seed of some dead person put to death for murder." With this belief rampant, it is no wonder the root, which is rare and difficult to unearth, would have such magical qualities attributed to it.

MAN IN THE MOON

Shakespeare (in *A Midsummer Night's Dream*) called it "This man with lantern, dog and bush of thorns, presenteth moonshine." Some people saw the moon's face as that of a peasant (usually with a bundle of twigs on his back, and sometimes with a dog). It was also supposed to be Judas, sent to the moon as a punishment for betraying Christ.

In Panama, the man in the moon was sent there as punishment for incest.

MARIGOLDS

Pick a marigold you didn't plant
And chances are you'll take to drink.
(Old English saying)

It is said that the marigold took its name from the fact that the Virgin Mary wore it on her breast. It is believed also that the flower sprang up from the blood of those who died during Cortes's conquest of Mexico.

In Western Europe and the British Isles the marigold has some unfortunate connotations. The Germans, for instance, say it is unfavorable to love. It usually represents grief, pain, or anger in other countries.

The marigold is intimately linked with the sun. It blooms all year, following the pattern of the sun, as it opens its petals early in the morning and closes them again by midafternoon.

The romantic Victorians modified the unhappy connotations of the flower somewhat by joining marigolds with roses and giving this meaning: "sweet sorrows of love." Mixed flowers with marigolds mean "changing tides of life from good to ill."

In Eastern countries the marigold, in conjunction with poppies, says, "I will soothe your grief."

MARRIAGE

See WEDDING CUSTOMS

MASCOTS

See also TALISMAN

The word mascot probably comes from a variety of roots associated with sorcery and witchcraft. The most popular modern mascots are those we see on ball fields: real or imitation animals that represent a ball team. It's an ancient and popular belief that a chosen mascot can bring good luck and keep the Devil away.

A mascot can be a person (a batboy), an object, or an animal. The animal mascots of today can be traced to ancient times, when there were animal totem poles endowed with godlike powers. These were believed to have a supernatural sense of good and evil and to be effective protection for man.

Zeus had an eagle as his mascot, which became the emblem of the Roman legion and later the symbol of Napoleon's army. Assyrian kings had trained lions and leopards, which accompanied them into battle, and cats rode with Egyptian warriors as their mascots. There is the Russian bear, the Chinese dragon, and of course, Uncle Sam. (*See* UNCLE SAM)

MATCHES

See THREE ON A MATCH

MAY DAY

You must wake and call me early, call me
Early, mother dear;
Tomorrow 'ill be the happiness time of
all the glad New Year—
Of all the glad New Year, mother the
maddest, merriest day;
For I'm to be Queen o' the May, mother
I'm to be Queen o' the May.
(Tennyson, *The May Queen*)

May Day celebrates new crops and flowers. It marks the time when cows are able to start feeding on fresh grass again. It's traditionally the day when dairymen are able to start making cheese and everything is in abundance. The Romans celebrated the day with parades followed by prayers of thanks to their gods.

The druids, who celebrated May 1 as the beginning of the new year, considered it their second most important holiday. Their most important tradition was to start a vast bonfire, as a symbol of the spring sun. Then they had the cattle walk through the fire to be purified. Lovers walked in the smoke of the fire for luck.

The maypole comes from the Romans, who cut a pine tree, stripped it of its branches, and then wrapped it in violets. During the Middle Ages, people incorporated the druid's custom of dancing around the bonfire into dancing around the maypole in honor of the spring crops. When the Puritans took over England in 1649 they ended the maypole traditions, calling them devilish instruments and forbidding the poles to be raised at all. After the Puritan reign, the maypole and the dancing returned.

Some popular superstitions about May Day are:

in England, the belief that to wash your face with dew from the
grass on May Day will make you beautiful
choosing the Queen of the May
"bringing in the May," a tradition of going into the forest and
bringing back flowers and branches to decorate the house

During the twentieth century, May Day has taken on yet another
connotation. It is strongly associated with the communist and
socialist philosophies. That concept started in 1889, when the
French Socialists declared the day to be devoted to the workers. By
the 1920s Russia had appropriated the day to celebrate communism.

MAYPOLES

See MAY DAY

MEZUZAH

See TALISMAN

MILK

See SPILLED MILK

MINT

This plant is associated with the legend of a young nymph named
Minthe, who allowed Pluto, the god of the Underworld, to make
love to her. Proserpine, Pluto's wife, became so jealous that she
changed the nymph into a plant. That is why, it is said, mint loves
damp ground and grows in profusion near streams.
Mint is believed to be good for stomach disorders and is used in
baths to calm nerves.

MIRROR

Mirror, mirror tell me
Am I pretty or plain?
Or am I downright ugly
And ugly to remain?
Shall I marry a gentleman?
Shall I marry a clown?
Or shall I marry old knives and scissors
Shouting through this town?
(Old English saying)

All mirrors are magical mirrors;
Never can we see our faces in them.
(Logan Pearsall Smith, *Afterthoughts*)

The Devil's behind the glass.
(J.C. Wall, *Devils*)

Woe unto thee who breaks a mirror: Seven years' bad luck without fail will follow. This belief is an old and important one in the history of superstition.

Long before there were mirrors, shiny surfaces were used to reflect images. These were considered tools of the gods. When ancient man saw his reflection in a lake or pond he thought he was seeing his soul or his other self. When that image was disturbed or broken he thought it was some kind of injury to himself. The Romans, at the beginning of the first century, added the time of seven years, the amount of time they believed it took for life to renew itself. (*See* SEVEN)

To break the cycle of seven years' bad luck, bury the pieces of the broken mirror.

Another popular superstition about broken mirrors is that someone will die in the family within a year. This idea may have come about from the basic belief that the mirror was a gift of the gods. A broken mirror prevented you from seeing the image of death. This was a way the gods had of trying to protect you from knowing that something bad was going to happen.

This belief has spilled over into several others, including:

Don't let a baby look into a mirror for a year or it will die.

Cover all mirrors in a house where someone has died so that his soul won't get caught in the mirror and be detained. It has also been said that the ghost of the deceased would gather the souls of all those who were reflected in a mirror and take them with it.

When a mirror falls off the wall of a house, it means death.

Witches and vampires are not reflected in mirrors because they have no souls.

A mirror which is framed on only three sides has been used by a witch to see over long distances. (I'd get rid of that one, if I were you.)

MISTLETOE

Kissing under the mistletoe at holiday time is one of the most pleasant customs we have retained from ancient times. The most pleasing explanation of this custom comes from Norse mythology. It tells of the goddess Frigga, whose tears turned into pearls on the mistletoe when her son, Baldur, came back to life. In gratitude for this miracle, Frigga put mistletoe under her protection, preventing it from ever being used for evil purposes. Since Frigga was the goddess of love and marriage, a kiss under the mistletoe symbolized her protection over the love of the two people kissing.

Mistletoe was sacred to the ancient druids, who worshipped it because it grew near the oak tree. (*See* OAK TREE) They believed that it reached the oak through a stroke of lightning from heaven. They used mistletoe in ceremonies, but only if it had been harvested with a golden sickle. They thought that the mistletoe would lose its holy powers if iron touched it. Because the druids worshipped mistletoe, it became bad luck for Christians to use it in churches.

There is another old tale about mistletoe that tells of priests harvesting it, never letting it touch the ground. It thereafter was hung over doors and arches as a sign of welcome to priests and as protection against witches.

To the Victorians mistletoe meant "surmounting all obstacles." That meaning came from another Norse legend in which Baldur received invulnerability from Frigga, except she neglected to protect him against mistletoe. An enemy gave the blind god, Hodur, a piece of mistletoe and told him to throw it at Baldur. He did, and Baldur died. Thus a blind man was able to surmount all obstacles and kill an invulnerable man with mistletoe.

MOLES

See BIRTHMARKS
CHARTS, Language of the Mole

MONEY

Money makes everything legitimate, even bastards.
(Hebrew proverb)

Coins date at least to the tenth century B.C. Carrying a lucky coin dates back to the time of Croesus ("as rich as Croesus").
We have these beliefs about money:

Finding a penny means that more will follow.
A jar of pennies in the kitchen brings good luck.
If a bridegroom gives his bride a coin and she wears it in her shoe at the wedding, it will bring a happy marriage.
Turn a piece of silver in your pocket on seeing a new moon and your wish will come true.
Put the first money you receive each day into an empty pocket; it will attract more coins (in English marketplaces this custom is still very popular; that coin is called handsel). This is an example of the popular theory of like makes like. (This is the same superstition as framing the first paper money received by a new store or restaurant.)
Another example of like makes like is the old saying that seeing someone with polka-dot clothing will bring you money.

Place a coin in a new coat, pocketbook, or wallet for good luck.
Coins with holes in them are thought to be especially lucky.
This comes from the ancient belief that shells or stones (once
used as barter) with holes were worn by the gods of the sea
and were especially helpful in keeping evil spirits away and
especially in preventing drowning.
Finally, there's the superstition about beggars and money. In
the old days beggars used to stand outside the churches after
services and ask for money from the worshippers. If someone
didn't give, he was cursed by the beggar. It is believed, even
today, that beggars have the power to curse people.

MOON

See also MAN IN THE MOON

If you think I'm going to tell you the moon isn't made of green
cheese, have no fear. That theory is too old to tackle; it goes back to
the beginnings of language. The expression comes from the meaning
of green as new or inexperienced. A new or green cheese resembles
the moon in shape and color. In *Proverbs* II John Heywood wrote:
"Thinke that the moone is made of green cheese . . . is a dolt and a
fool." (1500) Erasmus, in *Adagia*, said the same thing: "He made his
friends believe the moon is made of green cheese."
There are hundreds of moon superstitions, probably because the
moon, like the sun, comes and goes, and marks the passage of time.
It was of great importance to the ancients, and it provided easy and
convenient ways for them to explain certain phenomena. These are
some which have been passed down to us:

It is unlucky to see a new moon through closed windows or
through the branches of a tree.
It is unlucky to see the new moon over your left shoulder but
lucky to see it over the right shoulder; luckiest of all—to see
it straight ahead.
A robbery committed on the third day of the new moon will fail.
If you become ill on the eighth day of the new moon, you'll die.

If the rays of the full moon fall on your face while you're
sleeping, you'll go crazy.

The best marriages begin on the full moon, or a few days before.

A child born at the full moon will be strong.

A ring around the moon means rain or snow.

A crescent moon when increasing means good luck for travelers
and lovers (an effective amulet for travelers is a crescent-
shaped pendant).

It is a generally accepted fact that a full moon affects people in
peculiar ways. There tends to be more fighting, more crime, more
murders, and more fires during a full moon. In New York City in
1981 the police chief blamed a rash of bomb threats on a full moon.

The phrase dark side of the moon refers to the time from the full
moon to the new moon. It's also known as the waning moon and has
been particularly harmful to people throughout history.

The light side of the moon, traditionally a better time for people, is
the period from the new moon to the full moon. During this time the
moon is waxing, or increasing.

There is moon madness; you can be moonstruck or be mooning.
The word lunatic derives from moonstruck and comes from the
Middle Ages, when it was believed that the moon blanched the
brains and particularly affected mentally ill people.

If you want to wish on the moon you can try these phrases:

> *I see the moon, the moon sees me*
> *The moon sees somebody I want to see*
> (Presumably you'll name someone
> and then you'll get to see that person soon.)

> *New moon, true moon,*
> *Star in the stream;*
> *Pray tell my fortune*
> *In my dream.*

MOTHER-IN-LAW

Mothers-in-law did not originate with stand-up comedians. They were a serious problem even in early times. The Zulu say, "man should not look upon the breast that has nursed his wife." In old civilizations, mothers-in-law were completely shunned. Some American Indians have been particularly cruel to their mothers-in-law, since they believed that a man would go blind if he looked into the eyes of his wife's mother. One reason for this attitude was the primitive, deep-rooted fear of incest.

Happy is she who married the son of a dead mother.
(James Kelly, *Complete Collection of Scottish Proverbs*, 1721)

I know a mother-in-law who sleeps in her spectacles, the better to see her son-in-law suffer in her dreams.   (Ernest Coquelin, 1900)

MOTHER'S DAY

Near the turn of the century, Miss Anna Jarvis, who had dedicated her life to taking care of her mother, decided to launch a campaign to celebrate Mother's Day throughout the United States. The first Mother's Day was held in West Virginia (Miss Jarvis's home state) in 1908, and it was celebrated with a religious service. Miss Jarvis brought carnations to the service to make it more festive because they were her mother's favorite flower. Since it's political suicide even to hint that Mother is not the most important thing in the world, Mother's Day became an official, signed and sealed holiday throughout the nation in 1913 (the second Sunday in May was the designated day).

As early as the 1600s, however, England had been observing Mothering Sunday on the fourth Sunday of Lent. It was the day that all indentured servants and apprentices were given the day off to go home and visit their mothers. It was the custom in those days to bring along a gift.

Around the time that the United States began to celebrate Mother's Day, England took up the American version of the holiday, and changed the day to the second Sunday in May.

MOTHS

White moths are particularly important to the superstitious. For them, white moths (which only fly at night) are the souls of the dead. If the white moth flies around your head, it is the soul of a dead friend saying hello.

The black moth, as befits its color, foretells the death of someone in the house during the year. Perhaps this belief led to the invention of the camphor ball.

MOURNING VEILS

See also DEATH CUSTOMS

A widow is supposed to wear a veil during mourning to hide from death and to prevent others from catching death from her. Since the widow was the person closest to the deceased, she probably has some death vibrations around her, so she'd better conceal them. Death, you know, is contagious.

There is an old idea that close relatives must not wear jewelry or appear in public places for weeks after a death in case the evil spirits that had taken the deceased were still around. Today we observe some part of this tradition out of respect for the deceased.

MOUSE

Roasted mice help cure: measles; colds; sore throats; fever; and mixed with honey, make an excellent mouthwash, according to Pliny the Elder (77 A.D.).

The mouse is a bad luck omen in most places. If it eats your clothing, that is a sure sign of death.

It is believed that the Devil created the mouse in the Ark; or, that they fell to earth from the clouds during a storm. In Germany, witches made mice. In most places, mice make trouble.

*Consider the little mouse, how sagacious an animal
it is which never entrusts its life to one hole only.*
(Plautus, *Truculentus*, IV:1, 190 B.C.)

When a building is about to fall, all the mice desert it.
(Pliny the Elder, *Natural History VIII*)

It was discovered in modern times that powdered mice made a respectable cure for bed-wetting. (I'll bet!)

MOVING INTO A NEW HOME

Three removes are as bad as a fire.
(Benjamin Franklin, *Poor Richard's Almanack*, 1736)

A good luck charm is essential when moving into a new home. The custom is from the early wandering tribes who had a prevailing horror of the unknown and relied heavily upon charms and talismans to help them. Giving a housewarming gift is a remnant of this fear: a new broom, a loaf of bread, a used box of salt, and water must be placed in a new home before the residents can move in.
Other superstitions are:

Never move downstairs in the same building.
Moving on a Saturday means a short stay.
It's bad luck to move on a Friday. (*See* FRIDAY)
Moving on a rainy day means great unhappiness.
It's unlucky to enter a new house through the back door.
Move while the moon is on the increase, for good luck.
Always use something old in building your new house (used bricks or lumber from the old house).

MURDER

Other sins only speak; murder shrieks out!
(Webster, *Duchess of Malfi*, IV:11, 1623)

It is believed that the murderer's image remains on the victim's eyes. This superstition, which has haunted many a murderer through the decades and has been the basis of several novels, comes from the ancient belief that there is a permanent image of the last thing a person sees before dying on the eyes of the corpse (and a dead man always talks.)

MYRTLE

For the Jews in ancient times, myrtle was a symbol of the eyes, and so it became a symbol of atonement for lust (which shone from the eyes). To the Greeks, the myrtle tree was a symbol of love and was dedicated to Aphrodite. It was said that in Rome myrtle groves surrounded the temple of Venus and that after the rape of the Sabine women the Roman soldiers crowned themselves with myrtle in honor of the conquering of Venus.

In England myrtle is considered lucky. In Wales myrtle is planted on each side of a home to insure love and to keep the atmosphere peaceful.

In early Germany brides wore it to prevent pregnancies. (As a birth-control measure it didn't work nearly as well as the Crusades, which kept the men away from home for years.)

NAMES

See also CHARTS, Names

"What's in a name?" you ask. It depends upon whom you ask. At one time in history a person's name was as much a part of that person as eyes or soul. It was considered very bad taste to mention the name of a dead person because you might disturb the ghost. If you did mention the name, you always added, "may he [or she] rest in peace." Some people still say it.

The first Book of Samuel (written about 500 B.C.) says: "As his name is, so is he." Because of that philosophy, people have changed their names to bring themselves better luck and to confuse the evil spirits.

Having seven letters in your name is very lucky (either given name or family name) and people with thirteen-letter names should probably add one letter to bring them better luck.

"Change the name but not the letter, is change for worse instead of better!" (Chambers, *Book of Days*)

It was once believed that naming a child after a living person brought death to that person. Now it's believed that it will bring long life to the child. In some families it is believed that naming another child after a deceased one is dangerous, because the dead child will call the living one to heaven.

Then there's the Bible's instruction (in the Book of Exodus, 20:7): "Thou shalt not take the name of the Lord in vain;" so you see, this name thing can be a very serious business. People believed so strongly in certain ancient gods with several names that when protection was needed they said all these various names. The primary name of the god was saved for very dangerous situations. Otherwise, you would be using the name of the Lord in vain.

NARCISSUS

Narcissus, the flower of people born in December, was named after the boy who refused to love anyone, although many women easily fell in love with him. One version of the legend says that one day Narcissus saw his own reflection in a pond and was so enraptured by his own perfection that he fell into the water in an attempt to touch it. When his body was washed upon the shore, it had been changed into the flower we know as narcissus. The Furies wore these flowers as a crown to indicate their own egotism, the most fatal of all vices.

The word comes from the Greek word for numbness. The Greeks believed that the narcissus gave off a dangerous scent that caused headaches, madness, and sometimes death.

The Victorians failed to dim the unpleasant association of the flower. They acknowledged its meaning of egotism and self-esteem.

As a medicine, the narcissus root has been used in antiseptics and healing wounds. Mixed with honey it is used as a general painkiller.

NEW YEAR'S DAY

There are many customs associated with New Year's Day and its companion holiday, New Year's Eve. The New Year's resolution is the most ubiquitous of New Year's traditions. Wiping the slate clean, paying all old debts, returning all borrowed items, letting the past be forgotten is a very ancient idea.

New Year's superstitions are numerous. Starting with the evening before, here are the things you must do to insure a good new year:

Open the window a few minutes before midnight to let the bad luck out and the good luck in.

All debts and arguments must be settled before midnight.

It's bad luck to let a fire (in the fireplace) go out.

At midnight it's essential to use noisemakers to chase the evil spirits who have gathered in great numbers to celebrate New Year's.

Ringing out the old is an old tradition of ringing the church bells to let everyone know the new year has arrived.

"Auld Lang Syne," the song we all sing, is Scottish for "old long since," or "long ago."

New Year's Day has come superstitions all its own:

If you have no money in your pockets on New Year's Day, you'll be poor all year long.

Nothing should be removed from your house on New Year's Day; it's unlucky.

If you give a gift on New Year's Day, you'll give your good luck away.

Whatever activity you do on New Year's Day you'll do often during the coming year.

The person who drinks the last liquid from a bottle will have good luck.

Babies born on New Year's Day will have lucky lives.

Get somebody to kiss you. If you do, you'll be kissed often during the year.

NIGHT AIR IS BAD FOR YOU

Never greet a stranger in the night, for he may be a demon.
(Talmud, *Sanhedrin*)

Now the night comes—and it is wise to obey the night.
(Homer, *Iliad*, VII)

The night is no man's friend.
(Old German proverb)

The night has been associated with evil and death throughout history. Night air is believed to be poisonous and to carry infection. The night is believed to produce evil air.

The Romans believed that the air from the fields surrounding Rome was the cause of malaria. Actually it was the mosquitoes that festered in the ground outside of Rome that caused the disease. Even after the real cause of the disease was discovered and acknowledged, people still refused to go out at night, believing that mosquitoes bit only at night. Many still believed that the night air itself had caused the pestilence.

In Medieval times night was always a dangerous time for Jews. Evil spirits were everywhere. Tuesday and Friday were somehow more dangerous for them than other nights, and so they said special prayers for protection as they returned home from prayers on those evenings.

NIGHTMARES

See also DREAMS

Literally a nightmare was a spirit. The Anglo-Saxon word mare meant an evil spirit or monster that came during the night and sat on the chests of sleeping people. It stopped their breathing, creating bad dreams and an oppressive feeling. In the Middle Ages they were called night-hags. Then Freud got hold of them, and nightmares were never the same again.

NINE

See also NUMBERS

The number nine is frequently associated with magical things because, $3 \times 3 = 9$ and if you multiply it by any number, the answer will always add up to be nine or one of its multiples. For example, $9 \times 3 = 27 — 2 + 7 = 9$.

Nine often appears in ancient amulets. People wore nine stones in a necklace and on breastplates, and they tied nine knots (*see* KNOTS) in their prayer shawls.

Doing something nine times (like knocking on wood, or spitting, or turning in circles) is considered to have very powerful magic for bringing good luck.

Odd numbers in general are very lucky. Leases are often written for an odd number of years, like ninety-nine, for example.

NINE-DAY WONDER

Chaucer referred to a nine-day wonder as early as the fourteenth century, and a popular sixteenth-century proverb goes, "The wonder (as wonders last) lasted nine days." Another saying was: "Wonder lasts nine days and then the puppy's eyes are open."

Someone who causes a great sensation for several days, then goes back into oblivion is a nine-day wonder.

> *You'd think it strange if I should marry her.*
> *The would-be ten days wonder, at the least*
> *That's a day longer than a wonder lasts.*
> (Shakespeare, *Henry VI*, III:2)

NOT WORTH A TINKER'S DAMN (DAM)

This old adage seems to have two roots, both meaning that the object or idea referred to isn't worth anything at all.

The first comes from the well-known fact that tinkers (men who fixed things) had notoriously profane language and so when they said damn, it didn't mean much.

The second makes more sense. It refers to a tinker's dam, which was a piece of bread used to help catch solder and to prevent it from running through the holes in the pans being mended. Afterward the bread would be thrown away—since it wasn't worth a damn.

NUMBERS

See also: FIVE
NINE
NUMEROLOGY
SEVEN
THIRTEEN
THREE

> *There is divinity in*
> *odd numbers, either in nativity,*
> *chance or death.*
> Shakespeare, *The Merry*
> *Wives of Windsor*, V)
>
> *The gods delight in odd numbers*
> (Virgil, *Eclogues*, VIII)

Throughout history numbers have been assigned special powers.
The ancients attributed each number with a life of its own:
One meant reason; God; unity; and the sun.
Two stood for divisibility; opinion; sociability; and the moon.
Three (*See* THREE) had many meanings; perhaps most important, all religious symbols are in threes.
Four was imagined as square; the foundations of all things, as the four seasons and the four points of the compass.
Five (*See* FIVE) stood for fire; love; and marriage.
Six was a perfect number, since it equals the sum of 1+2+3; it represents creation.
Seven (*See* SEVEN) was a magical number, since the world was created in seven days.

NUMEROLOGY

This is a quasi-science, based on the rhythms of a person's birthday and the study of a person's name. According to Pythagoras, there were nine basic numbers and everything else was repetition. All compound numbers could easily be reduced to a single digit by adding up the values. For example, 502 becomes 5+0+2=7. All even numbers were female, all odd numbers were male, and the world was ruled by numbers.

The common conversion chart from letters to numbers looks like this:

1	2	3	4	5	6	7	8	9
A	B	C	D	E	F	G	H	I
J	K	L	M	N	O	P	Q	R
S	T	U	V	W	X	Y	Z	

To find the number for your view of life (the soul urge), add the vowels of your name.

To find the number that is the key to your daydreams, (the quiescent self), add the consonants in your name.

To find what you must do with your life, or fate (the life path), add the date of birth.

Here's an illustration:
C A R O L E = 3 1 9 6 3 5 = 27; 2+7=9
My soul urge=1+6+5=12; 1+2=3
My quiescent self=3+9+3=15; 1+5=6
My life path=1+1+4=6

NUTMEG

If you carry a nutmeg in your pocket
you'll be married to an old man.
(Jonathan Swift, *Dialogues*, 1738)

There's a notion from Michigan that carrying a nutmeg in your back pocket will help rheumatism.

You can also use nutmeg to remove freckles; to improve your eyesight; and around the neck, to prevent boils, sties, and cold sores. But frankly, there's no hard and fast evidence for any of these ever working.

OAK TREE

See also ACORN
          LIGHTNING

> *The oak, struck by lightning, sprouts anew.*
> (Ovid, *Tristia*, IV:10, 10 A.D.)

It is an ancient belief that lightning strikes the oak tree more often than any other object. People have planted oaks near their homes for centuries, to act as lightning deflectors. Some people simply keep acorns on their windowsills for protection. (*See* ACORN) A smart person, with a slightly superstitious nature, will not make the roof of his house out of oak planks.

The oak tree was worshipped by the druids, who saw it as a symbol of endurance and strength. They believed the gods lived in oak trees. (*See* TOUCH WOOD) The Celts also worshipped the oak as a symbol of their most highly prized virtue, hospitality. The Victorians also regarded the great oak as a sign of hospitality.

The Greeks dedicated the oak to Zeus, since it was an oak that shaded his cradle when he was a baby in Arcadia.

The Romans made crowns of oak leaves, which symbolized bravery and humanity. The oak-leaf crown was their highest award, given for killing the enemy, winning a battle, or saving the life of another Roman. Our military honors continue to reflect this tradition. "With oak clusters" signify that an award is for greater recognition than one without clusters.

OLD SHOES

See also WEDDING CUSTOMS

> *nowe for good luck, caste an olde shoe after mee.*
> (John Heywood, *Proverbs*, I:9, 1546)

The shoe is a symbol of fertility in many cultures. For the Scots and the Irish, the throwing of old shoes at all new ventures insures a fruitful conclusion to the endeavor.

In China a childless mother borrows a shoe from the altar of the mother goddess to make her fertile.

In ancient Palestine, Hebrews sealed the purchase of land when the seller gave the buyer a sandal as a sign of luck and fertility.

Today, at weddings, old shoes are tied to the back of cars to indicate that the rights of the parent over the child have ended, and that the husband is now responsible for the bride's debts.

ONCE IN A BLUE MOON

See BLUE MOON

ONIONS

See also GARLIC

Onions, like garlic, come from bulbs and have encouraged many of the same superstitions. In sickrooms, for instance, they are believed to draw the illness away from the patient; and cut in half and placed under the bed, they remove fever.

One sixteenth-century writer claimed, "The juice of onions annointed upon a pild or bald head in the sun, bringeth the haire again very speedily." Another early writer said onions "inclined one toward dalliance." Alexander the Great fed onions to his troops to increase their passion for war. Indian gurus think the onion induces tranquility.

The Egyptians frequently took oaths with their right hand on an onion, which was a symbol of eternity because of its spherical shape. (*See* CIRCLES)

Some people believe that dreaming of onions means good luck; others, that a sliced onion stops the itching of an insect bite.

The onion is famous as a weather forecaster:

> *Onion skin very thin*
> *Mild winter coming in;*
> *Onion skin thick and tough,*
> *Coming winter cold and rough.*

Sydney Smith offered this eighteenth-century salad dressing:

> *Let onion atoms lurk within the bowl*
> *And, half suspected, animate the whole.*
> (Recipe for Salad Dressing)

OPALS

See also CHARTS, Birthstones

> *October's child is born of woe*
> *And life's vicissitudes must know;*
> *But lay an opal on her breast,*
> *And hope will lull woes to rest.*
> (Anonymous, *Note and Queries*, 1889)

An emblem of hope and the gemstone of those born in the month of October, the amorphous, color-changing opal was highly valued in Roman times. There's a tale about Mark Antony exiling a Roman senator who refused to give up his hazelnut-sized opal. Opals were set in the crown of the Roman emperors to guard their royal honor, and so Antony was being cautious of the senator's ambitions.

The opal, like many symbols popular in ancient times, was a good luck amulet or an attraction for evil spirits. The Orientals even believed it was alive because of its changing colors. Long before Christ, the opal was among the most prized of gems. Around the fourteenth century, during the time of the Black Plague, it became an evil omen. It was said that an opal turned a brilliant color and then lost its luster when its owner died of the illness.

King Alphonso XII, of Spain, is said to have given his bride a beautiful opal. Shortly after she started wearing the gem, she died. The deaths of the king's sister and sister-in-law followed. The king started wearing the opal himself, and he, too, died shortly afterward.

In the nineteenth century, Sir Walter Scott's novel, *Anne of Geierstein*, which was about a young woman who disappeared after holy water fell on her opal, again gave the gem a bad reputation. Queen Victoria tried to bring the stone back into fashion by frequently wearing opals. With Victoria, however, it was as much an economic gesture as an expression of admiration. Australia was just then opening vast opal mines, but the stones weren't selling because of the bad luck stories attached to them.

The medicinal powers of the opal involve the eyes. They are thought to strengthen sight, cure eye diseases, and even make the wearer invisible. This last belief has turned the opal into the stone of the underworld, for obvious reasons. It is also believed that the opal is like the evil eye, and can invade the wearer's privacy.

The opal is said to turn pale in the presence of poison, to protect its wearer from contagion, and to dispel melancholy and sadness.

A blonde will stay blonde longer by wearing an opal necklace.

OPEN SESAME

This is a magical formula used to open rocks, doors, trees, and mountains. It's found in the story of Ali Baba and many other folktales throughout the world. Open sesame usually refers to the opening of something that offers wonderful treasures within, as in this early poem written for children:

> *Dear little child, this little book*
> *Is less a primer than a key*
> *To sunder gates where wonders wait,*
> *Your 'Open Sesame!'*
> (Rupert Hughes, *With A First Reader*)

ORANGE BLOSSOMS

See WEDDING CUSTOMS

OWLS

The owl was the constant companion of Athena, the Greek goddess of wisdom. Because Athens was her city, the owl was sacred in the city, and Athens was almost overrun by them.

The Romans, on the other hand, hated the owl, considering it a bad omen and believing that its hooting meant death.

Today it is believed that the owl can foretell the future and if one hoots or hollers near your house disaster is not too far off. It may even be foretelling a death in the family. So wear your clothes backward, pull out your pockets, throw salt over your left shoulder, and put a knot in your handkerchief.

> *There was an old owl liv'd in an oak,*
> *The more he heard the less he spoke;*
> *The less he spoke the more he heard;*
> *O, if men were all like that wise bird!*
> (*Punch*, Vol. LXVIII, 1875)

OYSTERS

See also APHRODISIACS

The oyster is believed to be one of nature's true aphrodisiacs. Along the lines of the ancient belief that like makes like, it was thought that the oyster, which resembles the female reproductive organs, would stimulate sexual interest. Casanova believed this and prescribed oysters as a sexual aid. Lord Byron in *Don Juan*, II, said, "Oysters are amatory food."

"It is unseasonable and unwholesome in all months that have not the letter 'R' in their name to eat an oyster," said Henry Buttes in 1599 (in *Dyet's Dry Dinner*). This idea came from King Edward III, who in 1375 restricted the farming of oysters from May to September

148   TOUCH WOOD

for conservation purposes. (During months without an R, oysters lay their eggs.) The idea that oysters are unwholesome in the summer comes from the simple fact that lack of refrigeration doubled the spoilage rate of the oysters and invariably brought food poisoning to the indulger.

Oysters are fascinating creatures. They are female during the spawning season, and then they become male.

PALMISTRY

The general idea of palmistry is to read hands in order to gain knowledge about a person's personality, past history, and likely future. If you're any good at this art, you can probably divine quite a lot of interesting information. Palmistry may be as old as the Stone Age, although the modern practice is based upon concepts from ancient India that reached Europe via wandering gypsies, who have always claimed an uncanny ability to foresee the future. (*See* GYPSIES)

Some notable people who have believed in palmistry were Alexander the Great, Eleanor Roosevelt, Aristotle, Balzac, Mark Twain, and Pope Leo XIII.

Palmistry is based on the shape of the hand, its size, the configuration of the fingers, and the lines and the protuberances of the palm.

PARSLEY

Parsley grows better for a wicked man than a good one.
(Old English superstition)

Because Romans decorated their graves with parsley, we believe that a gift of parsley will bring bad luck, illness, and even death to both the giver and the receiver.

Transplanting parsley is a bad idea. It brings bad luck, particularly when transplanted from an old home to a new one. Leave it for the new owners.

The Greeks, although they also sprinkled parsley on graves, believed it brought cheerfulness and good appetite and are said to have worn wreaths of parsley at banquets. This idea was revived in the Victorian Language of Flowers, which lists parsley as meaning to feast.

PASSING A PRIEST

The French, in some ways a curious people, believe it is unlucky to pass a priest on a country road. If they do, they will touch iron (*See* IRON) to ward off evil spirits.

PEACE SYMBOL

Perhaps our generation's most famous symbol has been the one for peace and disarmament. It is comprised of the signal flags for the initials N (nuclear) and D (disarmament). When you combine the two signals they form an ancient sign of man upside down, which means the death of man. Put that in a circle, which represents the unborn child, and you have a symbol that says dead children.

$\bigwedge$ = N

$|$ = D

"No Nukes"

PEACOCK FEATHERS

See also THEATRICAL FEARS

Peacock feathers are notoriously bad luck. The guy upstairs from me swore he had seven years' bad luck after he brought some peacock feathers into his living room.

The reason they are such bad luck is that at the end of each feather is an eye (some believe the evil eye) that watches you even in your own home, causing terrible things to happen.

The source of this common belief is rooted in the Greek legend of Argus, the hundred-eyed monster who was turned into a peacock, with all his eyes in his tail, never to be able to shut them again. The story goes that Hera turned Argus into the peacock because he fell asleep while on a spying assignment for her.

In the sixteenth century, peacock feathers were bestowed upon liars and cheats to signify they were traitors.

In India, the peacock was lucky because it warned of approaching evil, and it was thought to be magical. The Indians say the peacock "has an angel's feathers, a devil's voice and a thief's walk."

Since the earliest recorded times, the peacock has been highly esteemed in China and Japan. It was an indication of rank and a reward for achievement from the rulers.

The Peacock Throne became the symbol of the first Shah of Iran, Reza Shah Pahlavi (1877–1944). Nobody had told him that it was a bad luck charm, which his son, the second Shah, Mohammed Reza Pahlavi, discovered when his government was overthrown in 1978.

PEARLS

See also CHARTS, Birthstones

> *Liquid drops of tears that you have shed,*
> *Shall come again transformed to orient pearl.*
> (Shakespeare, *Richard III*, IV:4)

The unique gem that grows in the sea as a result of an irritation in the shell of an oyster, the pearl is believed to shine at night, to watch over the affairs of people, and to forecast danger, sickness, and even death by its loss of luster and its increasing brittleness.

The pearl is drenched in superstition and has at least two popular origins. The first is in the Scandinavian tale of Baldur, the god of light, who was slain with an arrow of mistletoe. It was believed that the tears of his mother, the goddess Frigga, brought him back to life. Her Tears congealed, and became the pearls on the mistletoe. (*See* MISTLETOE)

The second legend comes from the Orient. The pearl was associated with the fullness of the moon, which overflowed with heavenly dew, drawing the oysters to the surface of the sea. The oysters opened their shells and received the dewdrops, which hardened into the all-perfect pearls. (At least this acknowledges the participation of oysters in the production.)

Although it is doubtful that Cleopatra really dissolved her pearls in wine, pearls can dissolve in an acid wine or vinegar; however, this is a very slow process.

The Hindus believed that pearls grew inside elephants and were therefore holy.

Throughout the East, the pearl is a main ingredient in all love potions.

PHOTOGRAPHS

See also MIRROR

In many parts of the world it is considered very unlucky, even fatal, to be photographed. It is understood that a person's soul is in the image, and to take a photograph, creating a duplicate of that image, will allow the Devil to take possession of the soul.

When three people are photographed together, it is thought that the middle person will die.

It is unlucky for an engaged couple to be photographed together; why tempt the evil spirits into breaking up a good thing?

It's especially bad luck to be photographed with a cat, (*See* CAT) since that cat could contain the spirit of a witch.

To bring a curse upon someone, turn the person's picture to the wall, or upside down. If you turn it both upside down and backward, it's much stronger magic!

PEPPER

In ancient Rome, pepper was a status symbol. In the fifth century B.C., it was prescribed for female complaints and taken as an antidote for hemlock poisoning.

Spilled pepper isn't as dangerous as spilled salt (*See* SALT OVER YOUR LEFT SHOULDER), but it could indicate that an argument is brewing between two good friends.

If you want an unwelcome guest to leave, surreptitiously place a pinch of pepper under his or her chair.

If you have a fever, don't eat pepper—it will increase.

Pepper can't be all bad; Yale University was partly subsidized by monies made on the trading of pepper. According to *Reader's Digest Stories Beyond Everyday Things*, Elihu Yale worked for the East India Company, made millions of dollars, and then started Yale University with the money.

PINEAPPLE

To the Victorians, this pungent fruit stood for perfection. Given as a gift, it is thought to mean "you are perfect." It was enormously popular during the Victorian era, and a piece of prose from those days calls it:

> *So beautiful that it might seem*
> *to be made solely to delight the eye;*
> *So fragrant that we might be induced to*
> *cultivate it for its perfume only.*
> (Anonymous)

Although the pineapple may have declined in value as a precious gift in everyday life, the custom was revived temporarily for the 1966

Broadway musical *Cabaret*, which featured the pineapple as a token of love in the song "It Couldn't Please Me More."

PINS

See a pin and pick it up
All the day you'll have good luck

Pick up a pin, pick up a sorrow.

Pass up a pin, pass up a friend.

See a pin, let it lie, all the day
You'll have to cry.

Lend a pin, spoil a friendship.
(Halliwell, *Nursery Rhymes*)

Black-headed pins must not be used when fitting a dress.
Finding a safety pin is good luck.
A pin shouldn't be used to remove a splinter. Use a needle instead.
It's bad luck to give someone a brooch unless the receiver *doesn't* say thank you.
Pins stuck in a wax image of a person will cause that person pain.

Pins, because they have always been made from shiny materials, have always been considered magical. In early times pins were made from thorns and fowl and animal leg bones that had been sanded and shined. They were used to make clothing and tents.

Commonly associated with pins is spilled blood, because of a pin's ability to draw blood with the slightest touch. Primitive man was the first to put a pricked finger to his mouth to catch the blood. He probably wanted to get the blood before the evil spirits could.

Most superstitions about pins mention picking them up. That idea dates to the days of witchcraft, when it was believed that witches used odd bits of metal to cast magic spells. If you didn't pick up a fallen pin, a witch might.

PISCES

See also ZODIAC

Pisces is the astrological sign for people born between February 19 and March 20. Their symbol is two fish swimming in opposite directions, representing the extremes in a Pisces's character. The constellation Pisces contains two widely separated stars connected by streams of small stars. There is a legend that Pisces was created when Venus and Cupid became two fish in order to escape the fury of terrible Typhon.

Pisces are often dreamers and idealists, and because they are influenced by Neptune or Jupiter they are optimistic. They are also very adaptable, since Pisces is a water sign. The Pisces person is very imaginative and intuitive, and often a great creative talent. Pisces tend to be emotional and sensitive, and to worry about things.

The aquamarine is the birthstone of Pisces. Friday is their lucky day; five and eight are their lucky numbers; and lavender is a good color for them.

Some famous Pisces people are George Washington, Albert Einstein, Rudolph Nureyev, Frederic Chopin, Joanne Woodward, and Ted Kennedy.

Pisces, the fishes

POINTING

We've all been taught that it's bad manners to point. This comes from a time when it was believed that it was bad luck to point. People with the dreaded evil eye were thought to point at their victims.

Witches begin their chants by pointing at the accursed person. In fact, whole chants are recited while witches point at hapless victims.

POPPIES

Poppies are those innocuous little flowers from which opium is made. Can you imagine what ancient man made of this phenomenon? The extraction of opium from poppies was discovered in Persia and Asia Minor and was kept a secret from other areas for centuries. The narcotic effects of the poppy were understood early and are reflected in the ancient legend of Somnus, god of sleep, who placed poppies around a resting goddess who grieved for her lost daughter. When the goddess awoke, she picked some poppies, ate them, and then slept again, this time losing her sadness and sense of bereavement.

Opium was used for headaches and as a sleeping pill. Sometimes poppy juice was given to children as a sleeping aid.

In early times, the poppy was often offered to the dead. It was a symbol of death and its presence was considered a bad omen.

> *In Flanders Fields the poppies blow*
> *Between the crosses, row on row . . .*
> (Col. McCrae, *In Flanders Field*)

This 1915 poem refers to a belief that poppies grew on the battlefields from the blood of dead soldiers, a sign that Heaven was angry at the evil deeds of mortals.

The poppy remains a symbol of dead soldiers and is worn each year on Veteran's Day (originally known as Poppy Day).

POT OF GOLD

See RAINBOWS

POTTER'S FIELD

> *And they took counsel, and bought . . .*
> *the potter's field, to bury strangers in.*
> (The Book of Matthew)

We know that beggars are still buried in potter's fields. The original potter's field (mentioned above) was a plot of earth outside of Jerusalem bought by the chief rabbi with the thirty pieces of silver Judas received from the Romans for betraying Jesus. The land was set aside for the burial of the poor and the strangers passing through town. It is supposed that potters got their clay from this field before it became a graveyard.

PULLING THE WOOL OVER HIS EYES

Centuries ago the word wool was an accepted slang version of hair. In those days, men wore powdered wigs often made of real wool, and the expression grew out of the habit of jokingly pulling the wig over a man's eyes so that he was unable to see what was happening.

PURPLE

Remember the expression "To the Purple Born"? Since the earliest times purple was reserved for royalty and gods. Priests and other religious leaders also wore purple. It was a difficult color to mix, although it was used in very ancient times, made from the murex shell, which yields a brilliant purple.

The color became an imperial one and indicated divine right because of its association with the gods. Common folk were forbidden to wear purple until recent times.

In 1895 Gelett Burgess wrote this little ditty (called "The Purple Cow"):

> *I never saw a purple cow,*
> *I never hope to see one;*
> *But I can tell you, anyhow,*
> *I'd rather see than be one.*

Burgess and his rhyme became an instant hit. The rhyme was so popular that a few years later Burgess wrote:

Ah. Yes, I wrote the "Purple Cow"—
I'm sorry, now, I wrote it!
But I can tell you, anyhow,
I'll kill you if you quote it.

(Cinq Ans Après)

PYRAMID

The Egyptian pyramids, a wonder of engineering, have always seemed to say to the world, "we hold a secret." Many people have pursued that idea, believing that there was some hidden knowledge or even fortune in the design and construction of the pyramids. Alas, nothing has ever been found to substantiate these claims, but believers still look for clues.

In ancient times the triangle shape was considered the strongest for physical structures and was thought to be a sacred form. Many people took three iron nails, placed them in the shape of a triangle or pyramid, and had them driven into the front door of their homes to protect them from the evil eye, and later, from witches. (*See* IRON, EVIL EYE, WITCHES, AND WARLOCKS)

In modern times, around the outbreak of "Egypt-fever" in the 1920s, when the tombs were being discovered and opened, "pyramid power" and a con game called the pyramid game, took hold. It was believed that the shape of the pyramid prevented decay. People have reported that razor blades placed inside a pyramid lasted longer, that seeds germinated faster and were healthier; some people even claimed to feel better just being near a model pyramid. "Pyramid power" has never been completely disproved, nor has it been accepted as a scientific fact. The con game mentioned above was based on a chain-letter theory. People gave money, and as the base of the pyramid grew, the people at the top would receive huge sums of money. When museums began exhibiting the tomb of Tutankhamen in the late 1970s, both surfaced once again, proving only that people will believe anything if it's packaged right.

RABBIT'S FOOT

See also AMULETS
              EASTER EGGS

In the world of superstition the hare and the rabbit have become interchangeable, particularly in America, where the hare is hardly ever separated from its relative.

The special magic of these animals lies in the fact that they are born with their eyes open, which invests them with special powers over the evil eye.

The rabbit's foot—which, to be truly lucky, must be the left hind paw from an animal which has been killed at the full of the moon by a cross-eyed person—holds a lasting place in the hearts of the superstitious as a good luck charm. Incidentally, it should always be carried in the left pocket.

The rabbit's foot is considered a powerful charm against evil forces because the rabbit's strong hind legs touch the ground ahead of its front ones (a most unusual way for an animal to walk). To the ancients, this technique was so remarkable that they ascribed magical powers to those feet.

The hare was worshipped in the British Isles long before Christianity reached there. In witchcraft, the rabbit, like the black cat, was thought to be a witch in disguise. It was believed that a witch who disguised herself as a rabbit could be killed only with a silver bullet.

Even today, farmers watch rabbits as a weather indicator: a thick coat means a hard winter; a thin coat indicates a mild one. This has, however, proved to be as inaccurate a way of predicting the weather as checking onion skins or watching for the groundhog.

RADISH

John Seymour in his *Gardener's Delight*, tells us that the Egyptian pyramid builders were fed vast quantities of radishes, along with garlic and onions. "Maybe," writes Seymour, "they moved those huge stones into position with their *breath*."

The Greeks adored the radish. They even placed a golden radish inside their temple at Delphi.

The Romans, however, found it vulgar, treated it as a food, with disdain, and are thought only to have extracted the oil of the radish for medicinal purposes.

RAINBOWS

See also SMALL FOLKS

> *Rainbow at night; Sailor's delight;*
> *Rainbow in the morning; Sailors take warning.*
> *Rainbow to windward: Foul all the day;*
> *Rainbow to leeward: Damp runs away.*
> (R. Inwards, *Weather Lore*)

Coleridge called the rainbow: "That gracious thing made up of tears and light." Some think that a pot of gold can be found where the end of the rainbow touches the ground.

Others believe that the rainbow is the bridge over which souls are taken from earth to Heaven (or Hell). Some think that anyone walking under a rainbow will be transformed into the opposite sex.

RAM

See ARIES

REDHEADS

See HAIR COLOR

RED-LETTER DAY

The significance of red-letter days probably originated with the Book of Common Prayer. Saints' days and religious holidays of all sorts were printed in red in all early prayer books and church almanacs, and they still are. Our own calendars often have holidays and weekends in red, indicating that a day is special.

In ancient Rome, important days were noted down with chalk. Regular days were noted with charcoal, making them into black letter days. Red, a color which frightened the Devil and his witches, means good luck. Black-letter days are considered not quite so lucky; in fact, they're just ordinary days.

RED PEPPER

See AMULETS

RED RIBBONS

See also CHARTS, Colors

My mother claims she tied dozens of red ribbons to my carriage when I was a baby because so many people stopped to say how pretty I was. The ribbons were supposed to protect me from the evil eye, which spent a lot of time hanging around pretty babies.

The superstition is that for each person who praises the baby, another ribbon must be added. Each ribbon is a *kayn aynhorah*, meaning "may no evil harm you." (*See* EVIL EYE) Judging from the results, I'd say my mother's ribbons weren't large enough.

Another common superstition, following in the same tradition as the one about baby carriages, is to tie a red ribbon somewhere inside a new car for luck. This tradition probably comes from the ancient one of using a red rag to counteract bad luck and to bring good luck. Red, after all, is a color which frightens the Devil.

REPUBLICAN ELEPHANT

In 1870, the cartoonist Thomas Nast introduced a jackass into a cartoon that quickly became the Democratic donkey (*see* DEMO-CRATIC DONKEY), and so it wasn't surprising when Nast drew another cartoon, in 1874, for *Harper's Weekly*, which suggested a Republican symbol to the public. The drawing showed wooden boards, which were platform planks, being thrown everywhere by an out-of-control elephant labeled the Republican vote. The cartoon also included a donkey in a lion's skin, which was immediately recognizable to most of the magazine's readers as the Democratic Party.

Like the Democratic donkey, the elephant was not intended as a complimentary symbol at first, but it caught on and has remained with the Republicans.

Some historians point out that Nast did not introduce the elephant to the Republicans, that it was first used in the 1860 political campaign by Abraham Lincoln. In an August 9 advertisement, an elephant was depicted wearing boots and carrying a sign which read "We Are Coming! Clear the Track!"

RICE

See WEDDING CUSTOMS

RIGHT SIDE OF THE BED

See also LEFT-HANDED

Yes, Virginia, there is a right side and a wrong side of the bed!

The ancients believed that the gods lived on the right side of man and the evil spirits lived on his left side. Further, they believed that the human heart was located on the left side of the body, and if you slept on that side, you'd crush your heart and die. You had to climb into bed on the right side and get out on the right side, to complete a circle begun when you went to sleep. Going to the right symbolized following the course of the sun; going to the left, the direction that the Devil and his witches took.

Climbing out of bed on the left side (the wrong side) is considered so unlucky that hotel rooms are often designed so that you can't get out on the left side.

In the right-versus-left controversy, the Romans took the position that right quite literally meant dexterous or adept; left meant sinister, corrupt, or even evil. (Maybe that's why the people who believe in the political right always feel they're on the side of the angels and that the political left are nothing but a bunch of troublemakers.)

You must always enter a place with the right foot first. This was particularly important to the Romans, who believed that when you entered with your right foot, you entered with the gods at your side. If you placed your left foot first, you were in big trouble; the evil spirits were right there beside you. They believed so strongly in this that they stationed guards at the entrance to all public places to make certain that people entered with the right foot.

That's how the custom of carrying the bride over the threshold got started. The groom was trying to make sure that the bride didn't start their married life off on the wrong foot. (*See* WEDDING CUSTOMS)

RIGHT VERSUS LEFT

See RIGHT SIDE OF THE BED

RING OUT THE OLD

See NEW YEAR'S DAY

ROBIN REDBREAST

See also BIRDS

> *If a robin you should dare to kill,*
> *Your right hand will lose all its skill.*
> (Old Proverb)

Make a wish on the first robin redbreast of spring and it will come true.

There are two theories about how the robin got its red chest. The earlier version says that he singed it while carrying water to a good god caught in the fires of Hell.

A later belief is that the robin pulled the thorns from the crown of Christ and the blood turned his breast red.

In either case, legend has made the robin a special bird, with special reverence paid it by many people.

ROSEMARY

If you wear rosemary around your neck, you'll have a better memory. If you eat rosemary, you'll have an even better memory because, it has been said, rosemary stimulates the nervous system, which in turn stimulates the memory process.

In ancient Rome, students wore rosemary in their hair to help them remember their studies.

When planted near doorsteps, rosemary keeps witches away:

> *Run witch run, flee witch flee,*
> *Or it will go ill with thee.*
> *Run witch flee. Begone!*
> (Rhyme from Middle Ages)

Say that when planting your rosemary, or it probably won't work as well.

As a symbol of friendship and remembrance, rosemary was included in early funeral wreaths. Often it was thrown into the grave to indicate a special memory of the deceased.

A batch of rosemary under the bed at night keeps nightmares away and insures a sound sleep. (Probably because the witches can't get at you.)

Rosemary is such a miraculous plant that it was considered to be a cure-all for diseases of the mind and to make old people young again!

In the thirteenth century, Queen Elizabeth of Hungary claimed her paralysis was cured by something known as Hungary water, whose principal ingredient was rosemary.

ROSES

See also CHARTS, Language of Flowers

There's one tale that the rose first appeared in Bethlehem, when a young woman was falsely accused of a crime and sentenced to die at the stake by burning. Miraculously, the wood changed into roses and prevented her death.

It is also said that the Greek god of silence stumbled upon Venus, the goddess of love, while she was enjoying a romantic assignation. At the same time Cupid, Venus's son, came along and bribed the god of silence with a rose. This god of silence is depicted as a half-naked young man holding a finger to his lips and a white rose in his other hand.

Throughout history the white rose has represented silence and secrecy. The Latin *sub rosa*, under the rose, has been found in writings dating back to 479 B.C. It meant "you are sworn to secrecy." The white rose carved into doorways and above arches in banquet rooms reminded guests that whatever they heard inside was to be kept secret. The same emblem was once carved over the confessional, and sometimes white roses were actually placed near the confessional booths.

Roses have been the unofficial emblem of England since the War of Roses, when Henry VII joined York's white rose with the Lancaster red as the symbol of his unified kingdom.

Roses that bloom beyond their proper season are said to foretell death. The Romans sprinkled rose petals over the graves of the dead. The ancient meaning of roses was joy; today love has replaced that meaning. Every variety of rose, however, has its own meaning.

There's a marvelous legend that Cupid was stung by a bee while admiring a rose, and he became so angry that he shot an arrow into the rosebush, causing it to bleed. The blooms turned red, and thorns were created. Another legend has it that Cupid prankishly spilled wine over the roses, making them red.

RUBY

The glowing ruby should adorn
Those who in July are born,
They will then be exempt and free
From love's doubt and anxiety.
(Anonymous, *Note and Queries*, 1889)

Some early folks thought the ruby had the power of driving out evil thoughts, reconciling arguments, controlling passions, promoting tranquility, and preserving health.

It is said also to bring cheerfulness to its wearers, to protect against fevers, and to repel bad dreams. It is an antidote for certain poisons, protects against the plague, and changes color when an enemy approaches. It can also cause water to boil; but you need ideal circumstances for that to happen.

The star ruby is the most potent of the rubies. The gleam inside is said to be a good spirit.

The ruby is a particularly important stone in the Orient. It figures prominently in the Koran and is highly respected by the Hindus.

RULE OF THUMB

See also THUMBS UP

The rule of thumb is a measurement. It probably dates back to very early brewmasters who tested the heat of the beer with their thumbs to judge its degree of doneness.

RX

The symbol used to identify pharmaceutical prescriptions was originally the Roman astrological sign for the planet Jupiter. In the Middle Ages, when physicians believed that the planets influenced a person's health, Jupiter was thought to be the most powerful of all the heavenly bodies in the curing of diseases.

SAGITTARIUS

See also ZODIAC

Winston Churchill was a Sagittarius; so are Eugene Ionesco, Frank Sinatra, and Jane Fonda. Sagittarians are born between November 23 and December 21. Their sign is that of the Centaur or, more popularly, the Archer, which probably comes from an ancient Babylonian war god. Sagittarians are often enthusiastic, self-reliant, and outspoken, but they are not always as open to others as they may appear to be. They often don't marry, and they have a love for adventure and travel. They have high ideals, and quick tempers, enjoy life, and hate criticism.

Sagittarius, the archer

Sagittarians seem to have well-balanced characters, but they tend to be impractical. They are loyal and law-abiding, and they possess a commanding nature. Sagittarians have a tendency to gain weight and love an active social life. They often have magnetic appeal to others because they are cheerful to have around.

The birthstone of the Sagittarian is the turquoise. Thursday is their day, and the number nine is their lucky number. Purple tends to be their best color.

SAINT SWITHIN'S DAY

Saint Swithin's Day, if thou dost rain
For forty days it will remain.
St. Swithin's Day, if thou be fair,
For forty days 'twill rain nae mair.
(Old Scottish proverb)

On July 15, 862, Saint Swithin, the Bishop of Winchester, was canonized and due for reburial in his cathedral. It rained so hard on that day that the proceedings had to be canceled. It rained for forty days. When the rain did not stop it was decided to leave Saint Swithin where he lay. Actually, Saint Swithin had asked to be buried outside the church grounds, in the fields nearby.

SAINT VALENTINE'S DAY

See VALENTINE

SALIVA

See also CROSS-EYED

Spit on the ground to stop evil from getting around.
Spit loudly three times if frightened and no harm will reach you.
Spit into your hands for luck before a fistfight or any other contest.

Spit into the boat before sailing if you want good winds.

Mothers must spit on their babies whenever anything is ailing them. All complaints can be cured with saliva.

Gamblers spit into their hands for luck (just as the ancient Greeks did).

Spit over your left shoulder—spit into the face of the Devil.

It is believed that Jesus cured blindness using clay made from dirt and saliva. When the Masai tribe in Africa spit to say hello, good-bye, or anything, it means goodwill.

Saliva has always been the most effective countercharm against all forms of evil because it is a body fluid and cannot be faked. Anything found in the body is important in the world of superstition, with saliva holding a special place in lore.

Pliny the Elder said (in *Natural History*, Bk VII, 77 A.D.):

All men possess in their bodies a poison which acts upon serpents; and the human saliva, it is said, makes them take flight, as though they had been touched with boiling water. The same substance, it is said, destroys them the moment it enters their throat.

Any substance that can do all those things to a snake is pretty powerful stuff.

SALT OVER YOUR LEFT SHOULDER

Salt is pure and white—there is something holy in salt.
(Hawthorne, *American Notebooks*, 1840)

Salt was, for primitive man, a magical substance that could be used for both good and evil. Salt became protective against the Devil when it was realized that salt could preserve food; more than likely, it could preserve people. When salt was spilled, a special guardian spirit was supposed to be warning against some impending danger.

Because the common belief was that good spirits lived on the right side and evil ones on the left (*See* RIGHT SIDE OF THE BED), people threw salt over the left shoulder into the eyes of the Devil.

Salt has many implications. Foremost it is a symbol of sadness. The Norwegians believe that as many tears as necessary will be shed to dissolve spilled salt. In New England people will throw salt on a stove to help tears dry more quickly.

The historical circumstances surrounding salt are important for an understanding of the superstitions about it. Salt was, first of all, very scarce, very expensive, and very difficult to mine. Therefore it was extremely precious and was the favored token to bestow upon strangers as a sign of welcome; hospitality among the ancients was a far more important virtue than it is today. In ancient Greece, strangers were greeted with a pinch of salt placed in their right hands. In Eastern countries salt was given as a pledge against ill will. In Hungary, salt was sprinkled over the threshold of a house so that no witch or other evil could enter. (Remember, Hungary was the home of Dracula and many other vampires, and the people had to be very careful.)

Both the Greeks and the Romans worshipped a goddess of salt, which might seem excessive until you realize that they believed that salt purified the sea. Since they made their living from the sea, they lived by the grace of these gods. At birth, a pinch of salt was placed on an infant's tongue to insure long life and good health.

Because salt was so rare in ancient Rome, it was sometimes used as wages for soldiers, from which we get the word salary and the expression "not worth his salt."

Another common saying, "I'll take that with a grain of salt," comes to us directly from Pliny the Elder (circa 77 A.D.), who prescribed a grain of salt to be taken to prevent poisoning (in *Natural History*). It was his idea that to build up an immunity to poison, one should take a little poison at a time, with a grain of salt to help it go down more easily. Today, when we accept an exaggeration with a grain of salt, it makes the boast more digestible.

"He's the salt of the earth" comes from the Book of Matthew in the Bible, and it means, he's the best there is. When the Arabs say, "there's salt between us," they mean that something sacred has taken place, as a deal signed with salt in good faith.

Salt is still a sign of purification and hospitality in the East. In Japan, for example, salt is sprinkled on the floor of a wrestling ring before a match between sumo wrestlers.

In the West we continue to fear spilled salt, maybe because Leonardo da Vinci, in "The Last Supper," painted Judas spilling salt as a symbol of his betrayal to Christ.

SAPPHIRE

> *Wytches love well this stone,*
> *For they wene that they may werke certain wondres*
> *By vertue of this stone.*
>
> (Ancient witchcraft manual)

The deep blue stone known as sapphire has been worn throughout the centuries by kings, clergy, virgins, Hindus, and by those born during the month of September, under the sign of Virgo.

According to legend, the sapphire protected kings and other royal personages from envy, and it is thought to have attracted divine favor. The Hebrews revered the stone, because it was said to have been set in King Solomon's ring. It is the favored stone for bishop's rings. It is thought to aid in the fulfilling of prayers.

The Greeks dedicated the stone to Apollo and believed it was a good luck charm. It was thought to have the power to kill spiders, to serve as protection to virgins, and to be effective against the forces of evil. The Hindus think it is a very good luck charm and that it brings health, wealth, energy, and the blessings of the gods.

The sapphire stands for wisdom. The star sapphire is particularly helpful against sorcery because of the good spirits that twinkle from within.

> *A maiden born when Autumn leaves*
> *And rustling in September's breezes*
> *A sapphire on her brow should bind,*
> *'Twill cure diseases of the mind.*
>
> (Anonymous, *Notes and Queries*, 1889)

SCARECROWS

See also BIRDS
           CROWS

    Long ago two pieces of wood were nailed together to form a cross to be used in the fields as protection for the crops. Later, clothing was added over the cross as a disguise to fool the Devil. Modern farmers have continued the practice of clothing a straw figure to scare crows away (in other words, to protect the crops from evil). It is thought that the scent of people, which lingers on the clothing, keeps the crows out of the fields.

    There is a saying that a single crow is a sign of evil. Should you see a crow approaching, remove your hat and bow bareheaded toward the crow. It ought to work.

SCORPIO

See also ZODIAC *Scorpio,*
the scorpion

    The symbol of Scorpio is either the Scorpion or the Eagle. Scorpios are those born between October 23 and November 23. They are quiet people with an inner strength, sharp vision, and a deep understanding. They can be secretive loners who resist change. They tend to be courageous, strong-willed and idealistic, with a strong, healthy desire to succeed. They sometimes have perception bordering on the psychic, and they almost always have a deep survival instinct.

    Scorpios are influenced by Mars, who loves arguments. They are partial to Tuesdays, the numbers three and five, and the color red. The Scorpio birthstone is the topaz. Scorpios love to love, but since they find fault easily with those they love, they are difficult to love in return. Scorpios are either very, very good or very, very bad. Mystery intrigues them, and they love solving puzzles.

    Some well-known Scorpios are Katharine Hepburn, Indira Gandhi, Pablo Picasso, Grace Kelly, and Kurt Vonnegut.

SEVEN

See also NUMBERS

Seven has always been considered a special number. To the Egyptians, for example, the earth was represented by a four-sided house in which three gods dwelled, which added up to seven. This became their lucky number.

Seven really came into its own with the Christian interpretation of Creation:

The world was made in seven days.

There are seven days to the week.

There are seven graces.

There are seven stanzas in the Lord's Prayer.

There are seven ages of man.

Christ uttered seven last words.

Most of the above beliefs are ruled by the different phases of the moon, which change every seven days.

The Romans believed that the mind and the body changed completely and were renewed after seven years. (They also started the seven years' bad luck concept—*See* MIRROR)

Seventh Heaven is an Islamic concept, and it represents the best of all possible places. It is the heaven of heavens, the residence of God and his angels. There is also a very early Islamic belief that there are seven heavens, one lying right above the other, graduating in degrees; depending upon how good a person was on earth, he or she could say, "I'm in Seventh Heaven."

Seven is especially lucky to gamblers. (*See* GAMBLING)

SEVENTH HEAVEN

See SEVEN

SEVENTH SON OF THE SEVENTH SON
See also SEVEN

The seventh son born to the seventh son is thought to be doubly blessed. He is believed to be a clairvoyant, with natural healing powers. Throughout the Middle Ages, the seventh son usually practiced magic and administered the laying on of hands to the sick.

George Stimpson, in *A Book About a Thousand Things,* hints that there might be some basis for this lasting belief. There is a school of thought that believes the children of older fathers are smarter: They inherit the level of intelligence of the father at the time of conception. Coincidentally, many geniuses have been the younger child in a family.

Gypsies seem to be the only people who give equal credit to the seventh daughter of the seventh daughter. They say she always tells an accurate future.

SHAKE HANDS ON IT
See also HANDSHAKE

When two people shake hands on it, they are blessing their deal. The two hands form the sign of the cross, which is thought to bring good luck to any venture. It is also a pledge of good intentions.

SHAMROCKS
See also FOUR-LEAF CLOVER

The shamrock has been the emblem of Ireland since about 433 A.D., when Saint Patrick is said to have used the three leaves to explain the meaning of the Trinity to the pagans and druids.

A three-leafed plant very like the shamrock was greatly honored by the Greeks, who believed that Zeus's horse ate them for protection. It was also found on Roman coins and drawn on walls in Egyptian tombs. Many ancient civilizations honored the plant and believed it brought immortality, riches, and protection from evil.

The word shamrock is Gaelic, or at least comes from the Gaelic *seamrog*; or from the Latin *trefoil*, which means three-leafed.

It is solemnly believed by all good and loyal Irishmen that a real, true shamrock will never grow on English soil.

SINGING BEFORE BREAKFAST

If you sing before seven, you'll cry before eleven.

If you sing before you eat, you'll cry before you sleep.

      Sing while eating
      Or sing in bed,
      Evil will get you
      And you'll be dead.

In an interview after her divorce from Eddie Fisher, Elizabeth Taylor complained that he used to sing to her at the breakfast table. Well, no wonder she divorced him! Maybe the superstition that singing at the breakfast table will bring disappointment in love has some validity.

It's also a bad idea to sing while playing cards. You'll probably lose. But if you sing unconsciously while in the bathtub you'll probably have good luck.

Most of these ideas come from the Greeks, who very sensibly thought that being happy early in the day was not wholesome since you hadn't had time to earn your happiness. They also felt that expressing happiness (as through singing) early in the day would bring unhappiness later, because things usually work in reverse.

SLEEP WITH YOUR HEAD POINTING NORTH

This superstition is still pretty commonly followed. It says that the head of the bed should always point north so that the person will be lulled to sleep by the earth's magnetic waves, which are thought to flow from north to south. This idea got started when it was discovered that the earth was round.

If you should be so foolish as to place your bed with the head facing south, or if, like me, you don't know which direction your bed is facing, then place glass coasters under the feet to break the electrical current's flow.

SLEEP ON RIGHT SIDE

See RIGHT SIDE OF THE BED

SMALL FOLKS

See also DWARFS
            FAIRIES

For our purposes, small creatures such as gremlins, elves, leprechauns, and trolls will be known collectively as small folks.

The small folks have been around for a very long time. Usually they cause no end of trouble, but something always makes them a welcome sight. In fact, we often go looking for them.

Some common legendary small folks are:

Brownies: from Scotland; a very friendly species of small folks, they live with families and work around the house while the family sleeps.

Elves: from Germany; mischievous and often spiteful creatures who are believed to have no souls.

Goblins and Gnomes: basically French, they are household spirits who have bad tempers; they like to live in dark places but when in the mood are helpful around the house. Gnomes are particularly fond of mines and work there under the earth.

Gremlins: probably English in origin; these are associated almost exclusively with airplanes. They are blamed for all mishaps, no matter how big or small, which befall planes and for all the crews' problems.

Leprechauns: Irish by nationality; these two feet tall shoemakers are believed to be very rich and stingy; have great crocks

of gold, which they won't give up; and vanish at the slightest
provocation. (*See* RAINBOWS)

Trolls: Scandinavian; they can be either dwarfs or giants and live
in caves by the sea or in the mountains. Fishermen are said
to be terrified of them, and they are believed to burst when
sunlight hits them head-on.

As Batchelor and de Lys in *Superstitious? Here's Why!* explain,
"The best part of these small creatures is that they can be blamed for
all human ills, bad luck, and accidents which is one of the main
reasons why they were invented, of course!"

SMOKEY THE BEAR

The most successful public-service campaign in America has
been the Smokey the Bear campaign against forest fires. He was
quickly taken into the hearts of Americans and made a part of the
culture—even if he didn't prevent too many forest fires.

Smokey was discovered during a massive forest fire in 1950. He
was a bear cub separated from his mother, who was rescued and
began living quite happily in captivity, which was most unusual for a
grizzly bear. They named him Smokey because of the fire in which
he was found. Eventually he went to live in the National Zoo in
Washington, D.C. and was a great favorite of visitors.

When the U.S. Forest Service decided to use Smokey as a fire-
prevention symbol, Congress passed a law making it illegal to give
his name to any other animal. That's how Smokey the Bear became a
national symbol.

The current Smokey was adopted by Smokey Sr. and his mate,
Goldie, when it was discovered they couldn't have baby bears.

SNAKES

Some people eat snakes to keep young. But then, some people
will believe anything.

"Snakes change milk into poison," says an old Sanskrit proverb, echoing the age-old belief in the snake as the symbol of evil. After all, it was a snake that tricked Eve out of the Garden of Eden. That in itself is enough to have created a bad reputation for the creature.

The Egyptians couldn't decide about the snake. They both hated and worshipped it. It was the symbol of old age and wisdom; when seen with its tail in its mouth, it formed the eternal circle. (See CIRCLES) Because a snake sheds its skin during molting, they believed it was immortal. Combined with the circle shape it forms, that made the snake a pretty important symbol.

In India there has always been a snake cult. They believe that the souls of the dead come back as snakes, and so snakes must never be killed.

Historically, the snake has often been a phallic symbol.

A snake ring has long been a popular amulet. It is believed to bring long life and good health to its wearer.

Finally, the symbol of the medical profession is two snakes wrapped around a rod of harmony, which symbolizes healing.

SNAP YOUR FINGERS

See LUCKY BREAK

SNEEZING

Gesundheit!

How many times have you heard that? In fact, how many times have you said it; or God bless you; or any of the benedictions that save the soul? In case you hadn't realized it, sneezing is a breeze from Satan's wings; the Arabs believed that Allah created the world with a sneeze.

> *On Monday, sneeze for danger*
> *On Tuesday, kiss a stranger*
> *On Wednesday, receive a letter*
> *On Thursday, something better*
> *On Friday, sneeze for sorrow*
> *On Saturday, see your lover tomorrow*

On Sunday your safety seek
Or the Devil will have you the rest of the week.
(Harland, *Lancs. Folk-Lore*)

A newborn child is under the spell
of elves until it sneezes.

The Hebrews say, "God bless you," when you sneeze because they believe that at the moment of sneezing you are as close to death as you can be. They say that Adam sneezed after Eve took a bite of the apple, and he saw his own death.

The Romans used to say, "May Jupiter preserve you!" because they, like many of the early civilizations, believed that the essence of life—man's spirit or his soul—was in the form of air or breath, which lived inside his head. A sneeze could expel that spirit unless the gods interceded. Many civilizations, both old and modern, bow toward the sneezing person, saying, "May your soul not escape," with the gesture.

During the Middle Ages, sneezing was a very serious matter. It was believed that evil spirits were let loose with a sneeze, which could be dangerous to anyone nearby. With the Black Plague lurking around every corner, this fear was "not to be sneezed at." In this respect, sneezing does spread disease, or evil spirits.

The Greeks wrote that Prometheus invented the sneeze.

The Romans were the ones who started the belief that if you sneeze while making a decision, your choice will be right.

In the seventeenth century, sneezing was thought to be a sign of good health, and English hospitals discharged patients who sneezed three times—that, they felt was a sure sign of recovery.

The Book of Genesis says that God breathed into his nostrils the breath of life in its description of the birth of Adam. Well, reasoned early man, if life went in through the nose, wouldn't it be logical to think that it could leave in the same fashion? Couldn't a good, solid sneeze dislodge life just as quickly as it had begun? Therefore shouldn't a blessing be said to prevent the soul from being damned? Gesundheit!

SOMETHING OLD, SOMETHING NEW...

See WEDDING CUSTOMS

SPEAKING AT THE SAME TIME AS SOMEONE ELSE

See WISH ON A STAR

SPIDERS

> *A spider in the morning is a sign of sorrow*
> *A spider at noon brings worry for tomorrow*
> *A spider in the afternoon is a sign of a gift;*
> *But a spider in the evening will all hopes up-*
> *lift.*
>
> (Old proverb)

Spiders have a long and varied history in the world of superstition. It is believed that a spider spun a web to hide the infant Jesus in the manger when the messengers of Herod came to look for him, therefore it is unlucky to kill a spider or to disturb its web.

A spider mixed with syrup will cure a fever (the spider will eat the fever).

A spider in a walnut shell worn around the neck will ward off the plague.

If you run into a spider web, you'll meet a friend.

If you see a spider run down its web in the afternoon, you'll take a trip.

The daddy longlegs spider is especially lucky, and if a plow kills one, the cows will go dry.

It is said that Robert Bruce, the king of Scotland, watched a spider build its web for inspiration while he was held prisoner. Following the spider's lead, he freed Scotland from English rule.

The name of the dance known as the tarantella was derived from an old folk cure for the bite of a tarantula spider.

It was also believed that the Roman gods were jealous of the delicacy of the work that spiders did when spinning their webs.

SPILLED MILK

There's an old Russian saying: "Don't cry over spilled milk. If you would live forever, wash milk from your liver. What is taken in with milk, goes out with the soul."

Some say it's unlucky to spill milk. To counteract this bad luck, say your enemy's name three times.

If bubbles form at the top of a glass of milk (or a cup of coffee) immediately after you've poured it and you can drink the bubbles before they break, you'll get a lot of money.

Any spilled drink, in Ireland, is lucky. The liquid on the ground is a treat for the small folks (*See* SMALL FOLKS), and they'll repay your kindness.

SPILLED SALT

See SALT OVER YOUR LEFT SHOULDER

SPIT

See SALIVA

STAR OF DAVID

See also TALISMAN

The Magen David or Solomon's Seal, as the Star of David is known, is used as an amulet against demons and bad spirits.

In today's world, it is also the symbol of Israel and the symbol of the Jewish religion. It is made by superimposing one triangle, representing the male, over another triangle, representing the female. For very religious Jews, the true name of God must never be spoken, and so this star, which is thought to comprise the four elements of the universe, is used to represent God. Synagogues, religious books, and paraphernalia of the religion are stamped with this Magen David.

STARS

Whenever a mortal falls in sin,
Tears fall from angels eyes.
And this is why at times there
fall Bright stars from out the skies.

All wishes made on a shooting star will come true.
Shooting stars mean someone will die because they clear the path for a soul to get to Heaven.
It's unlucky to point at the stars; stars are really angels, and if you point you might poke their eyes.
Falling stars are the souls of children coming to earth, on their way to being born.
Stars are lucky; because of that, more countries have stars on their flags than any other symbol.

The Star of Destiny is a popular concept in astrology. It is believed that each person receives a Star of Destiny that serves as his or her own guiding star throughout life. It disappears at death. (*See* FIVE)

Stars are also special people with star quality. Noel Coward, when asked if he had something special to say to the star of his new play, answered, "Yes. Twinkle."

STEP ON A CRACK

The most popular form of this grisly saying is:

Step on a crack, break your mother's back.

It comes from the belief that a crack represents the opening of a grave. To step on that crack meant you might be walking on the grave of someone in your family. (This notion predates pavement, with its carefully measured squares that make it almost impossible *not* to walk on a crack.) The whole poem goes:

Step in a hole
You'll break your mother's sugar bowl.
Step on a crack,
You'll break your mother's back.
Step in a ditch,
Your mother's nose will itch.
Step on the dirt
You'll tear your father's shirt.
Step on a nail
You'll put your father in jail.
(Old children's rhyme)

STEP UNDER A LADDER

See WALKING UNDER LADDERS

STONES

See AMULETS

STORKS BRING BABIES

This is such a persistent legend in households that have small children that most of us half believe it even though we really know better—don't we?

The whole superstition is that storks pick up infants from marshes, streams, caves, and other such places where the souls of unborn babies reside and bring them to their new homes.

The stork has been observed to be a good "family man" for many centuries. Aristotle made it a crime to kill a stork in Greece in 330 B.C. The Romans passed the stork's law (*lex ciconaria*), which compelled children to care for their needy parents in old age.

In Roman mythology the stork was sacred to Venus. When a stork couple built their nest on the rooftop of a home it was considered a blessing from Venus and a promise of enduring love.

Veteran stork watchers know that each year the stork returns to build its nest on the same spot, and superstitious stork watchers know that means good luck.

It is a popular custom to say that when a stork flies over a home, a birth is about to take place.

STRING AROUND YOUR FINGER

Unfortunately, many people tie a piece of string around a finger, then forget what it was they were trying to remember. If they had tied the string onto a finger of the left hand it probably would have worked better, because the seat of all knowledge and memory is on the left side—where the heart used to be.

In the old days, the spirit of life often presented itself in the form of a body pain. The pain was thought to stay in one place if a piece of string or other fabric was tied around the spot. This also served as a cure for the pain. The string remained on the spot as a reminder of where the pain had been. That's how come we tie string around our fingers to remind us of something.

STY

An absolutely guaranteed way to cure a sty in your eye is to rub it nine times with a gold wedding ring.

If that doesn't work, press a copper penny to your sty then throw the penny away. The person who picks up the penny (a greedy soul) will pick up your sty. (If that doesn't work, see a doctor.)

SUCKER BORN EVERY MINUTE, THERE'S A

This saying has been ascribed to the circus man P. T. Barnum, and he should have known.

SUN

See SUNRISE

SUNRISE

> *Sad soul, take comfort, nor forget*
> *That sunrise never failed us yet.*
> (C. L. Thaxter,
> *The Sunrise Never Failed Us Yet*)

That's the amazing thing about the sun and sunrise—it always comes again the next day. It was a great comfort to primitive man, and so he worshipped the sun and feared its loss. An eclipse frightened him terribly. He believed, as many modern, more sophisticated people do, that the sun hides before every great sorrow.

Sunrise is a time often associated with death. More deaths, even through natural causes, are recorded at sunrise than at any other time. The unwholesome association of death with the sun comes from early man's worship of the sun. Sacrifices to the sun god were always made at sunrise.

Condemned people are traditionally executed at sunrise.

SWAN SONG

> *He made a swan-like end,*
> *Fading in music.*
> (Shakespeare,
> *Merchant of Venice* III:2)

Back in 400 B.C., the Greek god Apollo was said to have given his soul to the swan. When swans died they were said to sing in anticipation of the great times Apollo had in store for them after their deaths.

The final piece of work from a creative person is said to be his swan song, the last the world will hear of him.

Incidentally, swans don't sing before they die. They hardly even groan.

SWEEPING THE DUST OUT

This superstition is popular in many countries and probably falls under the old wives' tale heading. It goes: When you sweep the dust out the front door, good fortune goes with it; or if you use a broom to sweep the dust out the front door, you'll sweep your friends away.

One explanation for this is based on the belief that at homes fortunate enough to have good spirits living just outside the front door (for protection against the Devil), you would get dust in their faces when you swept out your home—and that's insulting.

TALISMAN

See also AMULETS
          CHARMS
          GARLIC
          HORSESHOES
          MASCOTS

In the world of superstition, people wear amulets and talismans for luck. An amulet is a passive protection against evil and the Devil; the talisman, is a more active form of this sport. You touch it, kiss it, or wave it about to bring good or evil upon yourself or someone else.

The cross and the mezuzah are popular talismans, as are other religious symbols such as the ancient ankh (*See* ANKH), saint medallions, the Polynesian tiki, and the fish emblem.

Let's examine the mezuzah because it, probably more than any other object still in use today, embodies all the principles of a talisman. The mezuzah is a hollow metal tube into which is inserted a small roll of parchment, inscribed with the central vow of Judaism: "Hear, O Israel, the Lord our God is One." This small object is then nailed to the doorpost of a home, consecrating that home and keeping it safe. For more active protection, each person touches or kisses the mezuzah when entering the house. The concept comes from the Book of Deuteronomy: "upon the doorposts of thy house and on thy gates."

Some scholars have indicated that the mezuzah is descended from the Egyptian practice of writing lucky sayings over the entrance of homes and gathering places. The Muslims inscribe the name Allah and print verses from the Koran on their buildings.

All doorways and entrances are invitations to the Devil, and so doorknobs and knockers often represent angels, lions, gargoyles, or other protective images. Throughout history there have been carvings placed over windows and arches for protection, just as garlic (*See* GARLIC) is hung over doorways, or a horseshoe (*See* HORSE-SHOES) is nailed over the barn door.

Talismans are often simple objects like coins or lucky hats that weekend fishermen wear. We mortals have such little faith in our own abilities and are so susceptible to the influences of the Fates that we will credit any odd piece of cloth or metal with supernatural powers in order to change what will, undoubtedly, be bad luck without divine intervention.

TAROT

The mystical tarot is a deck of seventy-eight cards used primarily for fortune-telling. There are four suits within the pack, divided into the Minor Arcana (of which there are fifty-six cards), and the Major Arcana (twenty-two cards). The Major Arcana are said to have been derived from the world's oldest book. They are pictures with very specific meanings.

The original tarot cards were used to predict the rise and fall of the waters of the Nile, which fertilized the lands around the river and therefore sustained the Egyptians. Some say they came from the ancient Hebrews. Others insist they were a part of Egyptian mythology. A large school of thought believes they came from ancient India and China via the gypsies, who added their own well-known fortune-telling skills to the practice of reading the cards. (*See* GYPSIES)

There is one legend which says that after Alexandria was destroyed, Fez became the most important city in the world. Wise men from all over came to compare knowledge, but they didn't understand each other's language, and so a book of pictures was devised. That book became the Major Arcana of the tarot deck. Eden Gray, in *The Tarot Revealed*, explains that the "symbols are the picture forms of inner thoughts; they have rightly been called the doors leading to the hidden chambers of the mind." According to Gray, "The magic is in the cards."

Actually, the magic is in the reader of the cards. A skilled tarot interpreter can weave wild and wonderful tales of futures filled with money, success, love, and good health or foresee a world filled with death, destruction, and hate. It's all in the eye of the beholder.

The Major Arcana, the important fortune-telling section of the pack, consists of twenty-two different pictures:

1. The Magician or Minstrel: skill
2. High Priestess: mystery
3. The Empress: marriage
4. The Emperor: control or power
5. The High Priest: convention
6. Lovers: choice and responsibility
7. Chariot: success in artistic endeavors
8. Strength or Justice: spiritual over material wealth
9. The Hermit: help and guidance
10. The Wheel of Fortune: good luck
11. Strength or Justice: balanced future
12. The Hanged Man: self-sacrifice

13. Death: change
14. Temperance: adaptability
15. The Devil: black magic
16. The Tower being struck by Lightning: conflict
17. The Stars: hope
18. The Moon: dreams and imaginiation
19. The Sun: material happiness
20. The Final Judgment: renewal
21. The World: assured success
22. The Fool: choice (also numbered as 0)

None of these cards mean anything by themselves. It's up to the tarot reader to put together the meanings of all the cards dealt to the individual. Each card has an auxiliary meaning, depending upon when it turns up during the reading.

The earliest deck of tarot cards still in existence dates to 1390 and can be found in a French museum.

TATTOOS

Sailors with bulging muscles weren't the first to discover the (debatable) art of tattooing. In ancient Egypt, women of high birth wore tattoos on their heads, necks, and breasts. Iranian women still wear them.

Tattoos on women were a fad during World War I, when George Burchett advertised his designs as "Dainty Tints Imprinted on Society Ladies' Cheeks." In 1920, an Egyptian tomb was opened to reveal a vastly tattooed princess, and Burchett's business boomed.

Sailors, of course, do wear tattoos. Some wear them as a sign of virility, and some believe tattoos protect them from drowning. Centuries ago sailors had tattoos done as protection against smallpox. Some sailors have tattoos printed on their skins just because they have nothing else to do some nights.

TAURUS

See also ZODIAC

Taurus, the bull

They say you can always tell a Taurus, whose symbol is the Bull, because Taurus people are strong-willed, with firm, almost unshakable characters. Born between April 21 and May 20, they are conservative people who are loyal and helpful to their friends. They are creative and are often active in the arts.

They are very good at solving problems, although it may take them a little while, since they get bogged down in details.

Taurus is under the guardianship of Venus, which makes the Taurus an attractive person, primarily a homebody devoted to the family. To the Greeks, the Bull was the disguise that Zeus took when he kidnapped Europa. It is the sign that indicates the beginning of spring, and it is an earth sign, making the Taurus melancholy and stubborn.

The best day of the week for Taurus people is Friday, one and nine are their best numbers, and blue is their special color. The emerald is the birthstone for Taurus people.

Some celebrities born under this sign are Harry S Truman, Shirley Temple, Duke Ellington, Fred Astaire, and Salvador Dali.

THANKSGIVING

This holiday was first celebrated about 2000 B.C., when the Mayans celebrated their harvest as our Pilgrims did when they held their party at Plymouth Rock in 1620. The Aztecs also celebrated the holiday, but they were more demanding in their rites than either the Mayans or the Pilgrims: They insisted that a young girl be beheaded as a sacrifice to the gods for the crops.

There is some evidence that the Mayans played games not unlike our football on their Thanksgiving. Even the Pilgrims are thought to have played stoolball on Thanksgiving, and so the football game at the college of your choice on this holiday is really from an ancient tradition.

Most of the ancient civilizations honored the sun and the crops with a fall feast. We know for certain that the Syrians, Egyptians, Mesopotamians, and Hebrews had special days very like our Thanksgiving.

Both Washington and Lincoln proclaimed a day of Thanksgiving in November (Congress made it an official national holiday in 1941), even though people had been celebrating it for years. There is no evidence that turkey, cranberry sauce, or pumpkin pie were ever served at that first celebration (but so what?).

THEATRICAL FEARS

A certain woman went to the theater and brought the Devil home with her. And when the unclean spirit was pressed in the exorcism, and asked how he durst attack a Christian, 'I have done nothing,' says he, 'but what I can justify, for I seized her upon my own ground.'

(Tertullian, 200 A.D.)

It's no contest. Actors are the most superstitious people in the world. (They are followed closely by gamblers, jockeys, and sailors.) Everything they do contains an element of chance. An actor thinks: If it rains the audience will be small; if the playwright doesn't die before finishing the play, I'll get a starring part; if the producer remembers my sister, maybe I can get an audition. If I'd read earlier they would have remembered me better. If I'd been taller (shorter, thinner, fatter) I might have been right for the part. If the taxi had been quicker; if the cat hadn't walked in front of me; if there had only been an apple to eat; if there hadn't been so many people at the reading . . .

An actor always looks for the uncontrollable reason behind why he didn't get the role or why the performance didn't go well. Otherwise he'd have to look to his own talent, and that would be shaking his already questionable faith in himself. Rejection, the bane of the acting game, must be rationalized. There are so many theatrical superstitions that it's amazing the curtain ever goes up.

Let's start with the things which mean good luck:

A bad rehearsal means a good opening night.

It's good luck to start a performance thirteen minutes late.

A cat is good luck backstage. The best luck is for a cat to make a mess backstage before a performance.

A rabbit's foot (*See* RABBIT'S FOOT) ought to be used to put on stage makeup. An actor must never lose the rabbit's foot—that would indicate a loss of talent.

Americans say, "shit," and the French and English use "*merde*" once during a performance, for luck.

It's lucky to fall or trip on your entrance cue on opening night.

The Barrymores believed it lucky to eat an apple before each performance.

A hunchback in the company is good luck.

Visitors to dressing rooms must step in with their right feet first. (*See* RIGHT SIDE OF THE BED)

Champagne drunk in large quantities on opening night, or any night, is good luck. If some champagne gets spilled on opening night, you must put your finger into the spilled liquid and dab it behind your ears (they say Tallulah Bankhead originated this one).

Saint Genesius was the patron saint of actors. He was thought to be a martyred actor in ancient Rome.

On Broadway a "gypsy" robe is passed on from musical chorus to musical chorus; each time the robe has some addition from the play it has visited sewn onto it. The custom began in 1949 with *Gentlemen Prefer Blondes* and continues among "gypsies" (chorus dancers) to the present day.

On to some bad luck superstitions:

Whistling in the dressing room means that the person closest to the door will be fired. There are two reasons for this superstition. First, whistling carries and could be heard on stage. Second, during Elizabethean times most stagehands were former sailors who could handle the riggings; they communicated by whistling to each other, and a wrong or confusing whistle might bring a sandbag or a curtain down on an actor's head. (*See* WHISTLING)

The last line of a play must never be spoken out loud until opening night. This line, known as the tag line, would complete the play and tempt the Fates into causing trouble. Because, by saying the last line the play becomes perfect, and perfection is not for mere mortals.

Never open an umbrella onstage. This superstition has been traced to 1868 when an orchestra leader named Bob Williams opened his umbrella onstage just before leaving the theater in the pouring rain. He went directly to the pier, where he boarded a ship to cross the Atlantic, and an hour later the engine of the ship exploded, killing Williams. (*See* UMBRELLAS)

Peacocks and peacock feathers (*See* PEACOCK FEATHERS) are especially unlucky to theater people. Edwin Booth called it "that miserable bird of malignant fate!" when his theater went bankrupt in the 1870s after a friend gave him a stuffed peacock for the lobby as a good luck gift. The old Bijou Theatre had peacocks painted across the auditorium. It was considered a hard luck theater until it was painted over. Then the theater began to prosper.

Yellow is an unlucky color in the theater. (*See* YELLOW) It was worn by the actor who played the Devil in medieval plays. Yellow roses sent to an actor means death to a friend; and a yellow dog onstage means someone in the company will die.

Green is a really unlucky color. It has to do with limelight. In the old days the light used on the leads was green, or lime, and if an actor wore green onstage the colors canceled each other out; in other words, you couldn't see the actor (a terrible tragedy for any actor). Villians were highlighted with

lime. Green is also difficult to light, since it turns muddy. It
is the color of the fairies, who get jealous if mortals wear it
and are apt to cause trouble onstage.

Never wish someone good luck before they go onstage. There
are several reasons for this: To wish someone else luck means
parting with it yourself; to wish luck is to tempt the Fates.
Instead of good luck, one often hears the opposite: break a
leg, or fall down backward. Actors are also told to "give 'em
hell," "be brilliant," and "enjoy yourself."

Cats are bad luck onstage.

According to the venerable Lunts, it was fatal to a performance
to pass someone on a staircase either on or offstage.

The words turkey and bomb are unlucky. Turkey is bad luck
because of an early play called *Cage Me a Turkey*, which
closed after the first act.

Opening a play at the end of the week is bad luck; opening on
the thirteenth is also bad luck. Both will cause a play to end
in financial disaster.

Finally we come to the most prevailing of theatrical superstitions.
This has to do with *Macbeth*. The play is cursed—anyone who has
ever worked in the theater will agree. It is even heresy to utter the
name of the play or to quote it while in a theater. If the play must be
referred to, it is called "The Play" or "The Scottish Play." It all
started on opening night in 1606, when the actor slated to play Lady
Macbeth was taken seriously ill and Shakespeare himself had to go
on in his place. The play, written on commission from the king, was
roundly disliked by its patron and removed from the repertoire for
fifty years.

Throughout the history of the theater there has rarely been a
production of *Macbeth* that has not been plagued by illness, death,
fire, earthquake, or another disaster. In 1849, for example, there was
a riot at the Astor Place Opera House where *Macbeth* was playing,
and thirty-one people were killed. In the 1937 Old Vic production,
the director was in an auto accident, the producer's dog died, the
star Laurence Olivier lost his voice; a twenty-five-pound weight fell
and almost crushed Olivier; finally, the head of the Old Vic died on

opening night. As recently as the 1981 Lincoln Center production, the lead, Philip Anglim, lost his voice right after opening night and couldn't go on for two weeks.

There is an antidote for foolish actors who insist on quoting *Macbeth*: Leave the dressing room, turn around three times, spit over your left shoulder, and then knock three times on the dressing-room door before reentry. Most theatrical scholars agree, though, that there's little hope where *Macbeth* is concerned; it's cursed.

THIRTEEN

See also NUMBERS
          THIRTEEN AT TABLE

As in many important superstitions, the number thirteen can be either lucky or unlucky. The Egyptians liked the number and thought it represented the last stage of earthly presence before going to heaven. They pictured a symbolic ladder with twelve steps that had to be climbed during a lifetime, each step representing another on the road to knowledge. The thirteenth step led to eternal life. Death was merely a transformation and not an ending, and death, or the thirteenth step, was to be wished for with some impatience.

There's a theory that thirteen became unlucky because primitive man reasoned that when you added up your fingers you got ten; then add two feet and you had twelve; after that came the unknown, or thirteen. Since the unknown is frightening, thirteen became a scary concept. But primitive man also believed there were thirteen moons (not our more traditional twelve), and if there were thirteen moons it must be lucky. So you see, a quandary formed even in prehistoric times.

The Hindus have been blamed for inventing the idea that thirteen people at a gathering are unlucky. (*See* THIRTEEN AT TABLE)

For Americans, thirteen is officially a lucky number. On the back of a dollar bill there is a pyramid of thirteen steps, there are thirteen leaves and berries on the olive branch, and the eagle holds thirteen arrows (for the thirteen colonies). Unofficially, it's an unlucky number, and that's why so few office buildings and apartment houses have a thirteenth floor.

If you feel uneasy about the number thirteen, then you probably suffer from triskaidekaphobia. It's hardly ever fatal, and it's never contagious. Just take two aspirin and go right on to fourteen.

THIRTEEN AT TABLE

See also THIRTEEN

> *A Riddle: "Why should Pope Leo XIII have been a very unlucky man?"*
> *Answer: "Because he was always the thirteenth at table."*
> (A popular riddle during Leo's reign, 1878–1903)

There were thirteen at dinner during the Last Supper and guess who was the thirteenth? Judas, of course; but the fact is that thirteen at dinner was unlucky long before Christ had a final Passover with his friends. In Norse mythology there is a story of an unlucky dinner with thirteen guests. Twelve gods were invited, but after everyone had arrived, Loki, the god of mischief, crashed the party. During the dinner one of the gods was killed.

If you find yourself at a dinner party with thirteen at the table, the only possible protection against someone dying before the end of the year is for everyone to join hands and stand up together, as one. That should help.

THREE

See also NUMBERS

We all know that things happen in threes. Bad things especially happen in threes. You know that if one famous person dies, two more will. We get three chances, we give three cheers, we have three strikes before batting out, and we usually get three wishes. Why three?

Since the dawn of time three has been a magical number for man. It represents the miracle of birth: Man plus woman equals child. All of life is represented in the number three: birth, life, death; or,

beginning, middle, end. These add up to the eternal triangle; the
deity; the Trinity. Almost all religions, no matter how ancient, are
based on a trinity of some sort. In ancient Greece three important
rulers were worshipped: Zeus (the heavens), Poseidon (the seas),
and Hades (the underworld).

Trinities can be seen everywhere:

Man is made of body, mind, and soul.

The world is earth, air, and water.

The Christian Graces are Faith, Hope, and Charity.

Nature is made up of animals, vegetables, and minerals.

The primary colors are red, yellow, and blue.

Jonah spent three days in the whale, Daniel met three lions,
and Peter made three denials.

Perhaps the two most famous trinities are: the Catholic Church's
Father, Son, and Holy Ghost; and Shakespeare's three witches in
Macbeth.

THREE BRASS BALLS

The everpresent symbol of the ignoble pawnbroker still hanging
over the shops of modern dealers was first used during the Middle
Ages by the Medici family in Florence, Italy.

Averardo Medici, legend has it, killed a mighty giant during a
battle against Charlemagne with a mace containing three gilded
balls. Averardo liked the legend and to perpetuate it, adopted the
three brass (or golden) balls as his personal and family shield. Not
long after, the Medici family, the richest in Italy, became the leading
bankers and moneylenders, and the family crest (the three balls)
hung outside their business establishments. It's still there.

THREE ON A MATCH

Never light three cigarettes on the same match. That superstition, which appears to come from World War I, is really far older and
encompasses more than just cigarettes.

In World War I, soldiers became very shaky about lighting three cigarettes on a match when they realized that while they were lighting up in the trenches, the match glowed long enough to show the enemy where they were. Lighting a quick one or two butts wasn't so bad, but the third was almost certain to cause death since the match led the enemy straight to the last smoker. During World War II, attempts were made to squelch the superstition because there was a sulfur and match shortage.

In very early civilizations, when a chief died, all the fires of the tribe were extinguished except his. The medicine man (or witch doctor or shaman) relighted the fires three at a time with a stick from the chief's fire that was believed to contain his spirit.

Oddly, the Christian church adopted this pagan custom, and during the tenth century the Russian church lighted three candles from one taper at funerals to help the departed soul into eternity. Since these services were conducted only by ordained clergy, it became bad luck or even taboo for others to light any three things on a taper or match.

THREE WISE MONKEYS

See no evil, hear no evil, speak no evil. This idea goes back at least to the eighth-century Buddhists in China, who often depicted this philosophy in a three-monkey drawing. When the Japanese saw it, they loved it and emulated their neighbors.

The Western world took to the idea immediately after meeting the monkeys when the port of Japan opened in the 1800s.

Monkeys were very plentiful in China. Their agility made it seem possible for them to put their paws over their eyes, ears, and mouth.

THUMBS DOWN

See THUMBS UP

THUMBS UP

See also RULE OF THUMB

An itching thumb means visitors.

If your thumb turns back it shows you can't save money.

Pricking the thumb with a pin or a needle is a sure sign some evil is coming your way.

A long thumb implies stubborness; a wide one, wealth

The position of the thumb at birth was a very important sign to the ancients. A baby usually comes into the world with thumb clutched in fist; as the child becomes more alert the thumb slowly gets released and moves upward. This was thought to be a sign of life beginning. Conversely, at death, the thumb relaxes back into the palm, or thumbs down, meaning death.

This brings us to the renowned gladiator games of Roman times. When a gladiator fell, the audience was asked to decide whether he was to live (indicating by thumbs up) or die (thumbs down). There was often peer pressure to vote thumbs down, as Juvenal (*Satires* III) explained: "They win applause by slaying with a turn of the thumb."

To us, the symbol of thumbs up usually means approval, and thumbs down means failure.

THYME

The herb thyme stands for activity and energy. It takes its symbolism from the Greeks, who believed that the perfume restored energy.

Its powers expanded during the Middle Ages to include strength and courage. Ladies-in-waiting and lovers embroidered the image of thyme on the edges of handkerchiefs to be given to knights before battles. The most popular design showed a bee humming around a sprig of thyme and carried the double meaning of activity and strength. (*See* BEES)

If a single lady puts thyme in one shoe and rosemary in the other, and places a shoe on either side of her bed on Saint Agnes' Eve (January 20) or on Saint Valentine's Day (February 14), she'll dream of the man she's going to marry.

TOADS

See FROGS
    WARTS

TOASTING WHEN DRINKING

Here's to the whole world, lest some damn fool take offense
I drink to the general joy of the whole table.
                    (Shakespeare, *Macbeth:* III.4)

What's all this nonsense about clinking glasses together before drinking? It's to stop the evil spirits from opposing the eloquent toast you've just made.

Originally the custom was to pour a bit of the guest's wine into your own glass and vice versa, to insure that neither had been poisoned. When poisoning began to recede in popularity, the custom was modified to simply clinking glasses to scare the evil spirits, and saying something like "to your good health" as a gesture of goodwill.

The word toasting dates at least to Elizabethan times when a piece of toasted bread was placed at the bottom of a tankard before the ale or wine was poured. The toast was thought to improve the taste, and perhaps it did, because it served to absorb the sediment that collected among the nonvintage dregs.

There is one other assumption about toasting, or raising one's glass in honor of another. The custom comes from a time when the Danish conquered the British Isles. The inhabitants were not allowed to drink alcohol without the permission of their conquerors and had to wait until the Danes lifted their glasses.

TOMATO

The tomato, found as early as 500 B.C. in South America, has a strange history for a common plant. The tomato was first exported to Morocco, where it was later boarded onto ships for Italy and France. It was known as *pomo dei Moro*, apple of the Moors. The French changed it to *pomme d'amour* when they exported it to England, and so by the seventeenth century the English were eating something they called love apples. In Germany the common name for the tomato is still *liebesapfel*, which means love apple.

With this exotic name, how could the tomato avoid being considered an aphrodisiac? The love apple quickly became feared by virgins throughout the world, who often would not eat tomatoes until they were safely married.

Around the 1820s, and for years afterward, the tomato was believed to be poisonous, and the cause of a great many illnesses that couldn't otherwise be explained at the time.

The Italians have evolved an intricate folklore around the tomato. Tomato sauce, they think, brings health and wealth. A large red tomato sitting in the window wards off evil spirits; another on the mantelpiece will bring prosperity. These beliefs of wealth and health have brought us the pincushion in the shape of a tomato as a talisman. Most of us have lived with this kind of pincushion, never dreaming it was supposed to be lucky.

TOPAZ

Who first comes to this world below
With drear November's fog and snow
Should prize the topaz' amber hue—
Emblem of friends and lovers true.
(Anonymous, *Notes and Queries*, 1889)

Cleopatra is said to have liked topaz because it reminded her of honey. Ancient princes wore this stone to bring riches. In the Middle Ages, the topaz, set in gold, was worn as an amulet on the left arm, to ward off enchantments and other annoyances.

The topaz is supposed to help cure gout, get rid of worries, and calm the mind. It is a charm against lunacy and sudden death. It will increase intelligence, brighten a dull wit, and insure faithfulness in your love life. The Hindus even believe it will prevent thirst if worn near the heart.

Scorpios wear the topaz as their birthstone.

TO RAISE CAIN

According to the Book of Genesis, Cain, the brother of Abel, was the world's first murderer and criminal. In early days, the name of Cain was used by God-fearing people as a euphemism for the Devil. To raise Cain meant to raise the Devil, usually through loud noises or by causing lots of trouble or mischief.

TOUCH WOOD

I rarely like to be any considerable distance
from a piece of wood.

(Winston Churchill)

I always touch wood before I make my entrance.

(Will Rogers)

They'd knock on a tree and would timidly say
To the Spirit who might be within there that day;
'Fairy fair, fairy fair, wish thou me well;
'Gainst evil witcheries weave me a spell!'

(Nora Archibald Smith, 1900)

The concept of touching wood or knocking on wood is almost as ancient an idea as man himself. It is supposed to ward off punishment for bragging ("He who talks much of happiness," goes an old proverb, "summons grief"). Long ago people believed that if you pointed out your good fortune to the evil spirits, they would be jealous and take it away; and so they touched wood.

In the days of the druids, it was believed that good, helpful gods lived in trees. People would touch the bark and ask a favour. When the request was granted, they would come back and knock again on the bark to say thank you.

Knocking three times has the additional magic of frightening away the evil spirits by the noise, preventing them from hearing of the good fortune, (See THREE)

TOUCH OF THE BLARNEY STONE, A
See BLARNEY

TOUCHSTONE
See TALISMAN

TREE OF LIFE (KNOWLEDGE)
See APPLE

TREES
See CHARTS, Trees and Their Meanings
    TOUCH WOOD
    OAK TREE

TRIANGLE
See PYRAMID

TRICK OR TREAT
See HALLOWE'EN

TRISKAIDEKAPHOBIA

See THIRTEEN

TROLLS

See SMALL FOLKS

TURNING DOWN A WEDDING PROPOSAL

When I say turning down, I mean just that. This is a custom from colonial days, when a boyfriend came calling with a courting mirror. First he'd look into the mirror, convinced that his image would stay on the glass. If the woman of his choice accepted his proposal, she smiled into the mirror; if she wanted no part of him, she'd turn the mirror face down, or more specifically, she turned him down flat.

TURQUOISE

> *If cold December gives you birth*
> *The month of snow and ice and mirth*
> *Place on your hand a turquoise blue*
> *Success will bless whate'er you do.*
> (Anonymous,
> *Notes and Queries*, 1889)

The turquoise is a stone we associate with the American Indian and his unique silver jewelry; but the stone was primarily used by the Turks (after whom it was named) and others in the Orient.

The Moslems often engraved messages from the Koran into the turquoise and then wore the stone as an amulet. The turquoise is believed to have the power to warn against poison and to draw all bad things into it, thereby protecting its wearer. It is also said to change color to indicate whether a wife has been faithful.

During the Middle Ages, when almost everything had a super-natural meaning, the turquoise was thought to be able to cure headaches and to make friends of enemies. It was a symbol of generosity, sincerity, and affection. It was also thought to preserve friendship.

Ever since the thirteenth century, the turquoise has been a talisman for horseback riders. It is believed that the stone can make a horse surefooted and prevent the rider from falling.

There is a custom that for good luck, a turquoise ought to be given, not bought.

TWINS

Ancient man was thoroughly baffled by the phenomenon of two children being born at the same time, with the same appearance, to the same woman. They made up all sorts of explanations. They said it was bad luck and drowned one of the babies. (If the twins consisted of a girl and a boy, the girl was the one to be drowned.) The birth of twins was sometimes considered good luck and a sign of the father's virility; or it could mean trouble and be a sign of the wife's infidelity.

The Romans believed it was a good sign, and so did the Egyptians. They both invented twin gods. The Romans had Romulus and Remus, who founded Rome; the Egyptians worshipped Osiris and Set. The expression by jiminy is from a Roman oath referring to the twin constellation Gemini. (*See* GEMINI)

Superstitions about twins abound:

> If a husband with a pregnant wife should spill pepper, he must throw some over his right shoulder or she'll have twins.
> A set of twins who marry on the same day should use different churches.
> The Romans originated the idea that the first twin born is the child of love, and the second is the child of lightning. They also said that the second child is the more favored by the Fates.
> Twins are never as strong as one child.
> After having twins a woman is sterile.
> A red streak down the middle of a pregnant woman's stomach means she'll have twins.
> A set of twins only has one soul.

TWO-DOLLAR BILL

The two-dollar bill, a purely American item, has never been very popular with the public. It has always been considered bad luck and each time the Treasury department tries to reintroduce it to the public, it bombs. Fear of the two-dollar bill may have been started by gamblers, who have always equated the deuce with the Devil.

It is said that by tearing off a triangular piece from the corner of the bill the magical number of three (*See* THREE) is created as a countercharm to the bad luck of the deuce. When all four corners have been torn off, the next person who receives the bill is supposed to tear it up.

Some people are less drastic with the currency. They merely kiss it, since saliva (*See* SALIVA) is a very strong countercharm and usually keeps the Devil away.

TYING THE KNOT

See KNOTS

UMBRELLAS

See also THEATRICAL FEARS

It is unlucky to open an umbrella in the house.

If you leave your umbrella home, it will rain.

The first of these superstitions, not opening an umbrella indoors, comes from the very early (eleventh-century) idea that it was an insult to the sun to open an umbrella in the shade (especially indoors). The umbrella had originally been designed as a protection against the rays of the sun and was used this way for many centuries. It wasn't until the eighteenth century, when the umbrella came from Greece to the Continent, that it was used to protect against rain.

The pharaohs of ancient Egypt used umbrellas and considered them status symbols. They were particularly important in the protocol of the Orient, where umbrellas were a sign of royalty. One emperor of Japan had twenty-four umbrella bearers in a procession to show his absolute power.

By the sixteenth century the pope was using them, and it was said that unless the pope had conferred rank upon someone that person couldn't use an umbrella. An umbrella is still part of the pope's formal ensemble.

In the eighteenth century, umbrellas were often called Robinsons, after the one fashioned by Robinson Crusoe in the Daniel Defoe novel. Umbrellas were manufactured in earnest in England in the late 1700s and were often decorated with acorns (*See* ACORN) as protection against lightning.

UNCLE REMUS

See BRER RABBIT

UNCLE SAM

See also MASCOTS

Uncle Sam, the tall, skinny man in top hat and red-white-and-blue satin dress suit, and usually sporting a white goatee, has become the mascot of America. He started life, however, as Samuel Wilson, a meat inspector during the War of 1812. Legend has it that a group of visitors to Elbert Anderson's meat-packing plant noticed that the supplies were stamped EA-US and asked the inspector what that stood for. Wilson is supposed to have answered that the EA was for Elbert Anderson, the contractor, and the US was for Uncle Sam. The conversation was repeated and the nickname caught on.

The name first appeared in print on Sept. 7, 1813 in the *Troy* (New York) *Post*.

UNDER LADDERS

See WALKING UNDER LADDERS

UNICORNS

The unicorn is probably a mythical creation; but who's to say? There was talk of the unicorn during the Middle Ages in places like France and China. Biblical legend implies that the unicorn is now extinct because it was thrown out of the Ark.

We know what it looks like: kind of like a horse, but with a single horn growing out of the middle of its head. We think of it as a symbol of chastity, fierceness, virginity, and meekness (because it is said that the meek and the unicorn will inherit the earth).

The horn of the unicorn was said to be white at the base and black in the center, with a red tip. The horn could be used to purify water and detect poison. When ground it became a powerful ingredient in medicines. Ground unicorn horn was also reputed to be a very good aphrodisiac.

UP TO SNUFF

The snuff in up to snuff has nothing to do with the powdered tobacco people used to inhale for stimulation or enjoyment. Up to snuff used to mean a person had a highly developed ability to follow a scent or a clue because of his or her acute awareness. Today we generally mean a person who is well informed and not easily deceived (nothing very mysterious in this).

USHERS

See WEDDING CUSTOMS

VALENTINE

> *To-morrow is Saint Valentine's day.*
> *All in the morning betime,*
> *And I a maid at your window,*
> *To be your Valentine.*
>
> (Shakespeare,
> *Hamlet, Prince of Denmark*)

By tradition February 14 was the day that birds chose their mates for the year to come. If you should see any of these birds on Saint Valentine's Day it will indicate something about your future love life, as this little chart indicates:

> Blackbird: clergy
> Redbreast: sailor
> Goldfinch: millionaire
> Yellowbird: reasonable riches
> Sparrow: love in a cottage
> Bluebird: poverty
> Crossbill: quarrelsome
> Wryneck: no marriage
> Flock of doves: good luck in every way

There is an old legend from about 240 A.D. that tells of two Christians named Valentine who were martyred on the same day,

February 14. One was a bishop, the other a priest. Both were later canonized.

One popular superstition about Saint Valentine's Day is that the first person of the opposite sex that you meet that day and kiss will be your valentine all year long.

VAMPIRES

If you believe in vampires, then you believe that:

A vampire can never rest and is doomed to roam the world in search of blood, which keeps him in his semistate of being undead.

A vampire must be home before daylight and at rest in his coffin of earth by the time the first rays of light are in the sky.

Anyone who is bitten by a vampire will become a vampire upon death.

The only effective defenses against vampires are the cross, garlic, light, iron, and bells.

A body buried with an open mouth will become a vampire.

If a vampire is suspected to have seized a body, the corpse must be dug up, and if it is not decomposed and has good color, with perhaps some drops of blood around the mouth, then you must drive a wooden stake through the heart to help that soul rest in peace. (The instructions are very specific about this procedure.)

Vampires are believed to exist in many countries. They are particularly popular in Slavic nations and especially in Hungary, Dracula's home. Dracula, the world's most famous vampire, actually did exist as Vlad the Great, a terrible and bloody ruler of Hungary during the Middle Ages.

We use the word vampire today to indicate that a person is a bloodsucker, a greedy chap who preys on others. Another use of the word is in vamp, meaning a femme fatale.

VEIL

See MOURNING VEILS
    WEDDING CUSTOMS

VIOLETS

That which above all others yields the sweetest smell in the air is the violet.
                    (Bacon, *Essays*, XLVI, 1625)

The discovery of the violet is attributed to several sources. There are at least three Greek legends which give conflicting information:

Orpheus's lyre was resting on the grass, and when he picked it up, violets had grown under it.

Jupiter turned Io, whom he loved, into a white heifer to save her from Juno's jealousy, and then he created white violets for her to eat.

Venus was envious of Cupid's love for white violets, and so she turned them purple.

The violet was the symbol of the city of Athens. The Greeks used it extensively in their treatment of headaches and sleeplessness. The Persians crushed it for wine and the followers of Muhammad worshipped it. Medieval priests are supposed to have cultivated violets in their monastery gardens because they were powerful against evil spirits, and they used them to relieve swelling, hoarseness, and thirst.

Napoleon was known as Corporal Violette because he used the flower as his badge of honor during his exile. Consequently, the violet was banned in France for many years after Waterloo.

The blue violet is said to represent faithfulness and love; the purple variety, to mean "you occupy my thoughts"; and the wild violet, to be love in idleness.

The violet generally indicates modesty. It is the flower of those born in the month of February. It is currently used as an ingredient in treatments against inflammation and some cancers.

VIRGO

See also ZODIAC

Virgo, the virgin

Virgo the Virgin, or the Maiden, is usually pictured in a flowing gown carrying a palm leaf in her right hand and a staff of wheat in her left. Virgos are those born between August 23 and September 22. They tend to be very sure of themselves; in fact, they appear aloof or snobbish to many. They are dependable people, perfectionists, and hard workers who try to improve already established ideas rather than invent new ones. They are loyal, practical, and good with pets.

Virgo is the sign of purity, truth, and honor. Because they are under the influence of Mercury, Virgos are clear thinkers. Their birthstone is the sapphire, their best day is Wednesday, and their lucky numbers are four and eight. They should wear the color gray.

One legend is that the sphinx at Gaza was modeled with the head of Virgo and the body of Leo. In the Western world Virgo has been nicknamed the Frigid Maiden because of a seemingly untouchable quality.

Some famous Virgos are Leonard Bernstein, Raquel Welch, Ingrid Bergman, Ray Charles, H. G. Wells, Grandma Moses, and Nietzsche.

V SIGN

The V-sign is the symbol of the unconquerable will of the occupied territories, and a portent of the fate awaiting the Nazi tyranny.
(Winston Churchill, July 20, 1941)

As much as he might have liked to take credit for it, Winston Churchill did not invent the V sign. The Egyptians used it in amulets for centuries. It represents a god of ladders and staircases who, in gratitude for being saved from darkness, allowed the use of his powerful fingers as a support for faith and courage and to use for escapes. The Egyptians also believed the V (and the U shape) was a symbol of the continuity of life.

The difference between Churchill's V and some earlier ones was the direction. In the world of witchcraft, the inverted V symbolizes the Devil and his horns. Making the sign with the fingers pointing down means the Devil must stay down below where he belongs. Some people believe if you do this every morning when you get up the Devil will stay away from you all day long.

Some say Churchill didn't bring the V sign to England during World War II—the Belgians did. It is said that the sign was used as an identifying symbol among Belgian freedom fighters and that eventually a Belgian refugee introduced it on the BBC during a broadcast. In any case, Churchill could claim to have popularized it.

VULNERABLE SPOT

See ACHILLES' HEEL

WAKES

See also DEATH CUSTOMS

Sitting up with the dead was an ancient custom. It was also a time when heavy drinking was definitely encouraged. Time hasn't changed things much.

The ancients consumed vast amounts of wine because they believed that the spirits in the wine helped the soul of the deceased on its way to the spiritual world. They also believed that the wine helped to cleanse the sins of the deceased.

Watching over the corpse, one of the major reasons for a wake, comes from the notion that evil spirits from the underworld might sneak in and snatch the body before the soul has a chance to try its luck at Heaven's gates. Those who gather at a wake often sing, toast each other loudly, tell jokes, and laugh in keeping with the old beliefs that these boisterous ways will keep the evil spirits away.

This behavior, which some might consider unseemly, is believed by the Irish to make a proper and fitting send-off.

WALKING UNDER LADDERS

After you've spilled the salt and allowed a black cat to cross your path; after you've sneezed and crossed your fingers for luck; and after you've been foolish enough to sign a contract on Friday the Thirteenth, the only thing left to do is walk under a ladder. Then you've touched on most of the major superstitions.

Why do you suppose walking under a ladder would bring bad luck? There is a primitive belief that a leaning ladder formed a triangle or a pyramid, which was the universal symbol of life. Anyone walking through that sacred triangle would be punished.

In Asian countries criminals are actually hung from a leaning ladder instead of an opened ladder, because it is believed that death is contagious and that people walking under the ladder would meet the ghost of the hanged person and catch death there.

The Egyptians considered the ladder a good luck sign. Their legends tell of the sun god Osiris using a ladder to escape when captured by the spirit of darkness. Today many Egyptians carry miniature ladders as amulets for luck.

If you should walk under a ladder there are four things you can do to stop the inevitable bad luck:

Quickly make a wish while still under the ladder.
Cross your fingers until you see a dog.
Make the fig sign. (*See* FIG SIGN)
Walk backward through the ladder to where you started your ill-fated walk.

WALNUT

A very confusing history surrounds the walnut. In ancient Rome and Greece it was believed that stewed walnuts encouraged fertility. In Rumania, however, a bride who wants to remain childless places a roasted walnut into her bodice, one for each year she doesn't want to bear children. After the wedding ceremony, she buries the walnuts.

Legend has it that during the great flood God was eating walnuts. Those who were meant to be saved climbed into the walnut shells that God had discarded and sailed safely away.

There are tales of witches and evil spirits gathering under walnut trees. There's also a superstition about placing a walnut under a witch's chair so that she will become rooted to the spot.

A walnut branch is believed to be protection against lightning.

In medicine, the powers of the walnut are associated with diseases of the head. Walnuts are believed to cure anything from sore throats to thinning hair.

The black walnut has a batch of legends all its own. It was believed, particularly in England, that black walnuts contaminated apple trees. The leaves are thought to keep away ants and houseflies, and some American Indians used the bark as a very strong laxative.

WARTS

See also FROGS

Warts are mysterious things. They seem to come and go without much reason. Because of their mysterious behavior, the ancients had problems understanding them. It was said that toads and frogs caused warts. People came to this conclusion because toads have wartlike skin, and people firmly believed that like makes like.

The cures for warts are as old as the causes:

Pliny the Elder, in his *Natural History* suggested,

> *Lie on your back along a boundary line*
> *on the twentieth day of the moon, extend*
> *the hands over the head, and with*
> *whatever thing you grasp when so*
> *doing rub the warts, and they disappear.*

Steal a piece of meat, rub the wart with the meat, then bury the meat.

While a funeral procession passes, rub the wart and the wart will pass after it has rained nine times.

Tie a red string (*See* RED RIBBONS) around the wart, wrapping it three times.

WEATHER

Throughout this book there are references to weather forecasting. Every time a bird chirps or an onion grows a thick skin, someone says the weather will be either good or bad. When a cat walks this way or that, when a baby cries or a bat flies, there will either be a storm or fair weather. We all want to know what the weather will be, and the ancients, who were at the mercy of the elements in a much more real sense than we are, were especially anxious to read signs of approaching weather conditions.

Virgil in *The Aeneid*, claimed the sun was the best forecaster:

> *The sun who never lies,*
> *Foretells the change of weather*
> *In the skies.*

It will rain:

if a frog sings loudly.
if a bat flies into your house.
if the cows refuse to go to the pastures.
when the cat licks its fur against the grain.
when the donkeys bray.
when a pig carries straw in its mouth.

> *Swallows fly high: clear blue sky.*
> *Swallows fly high: rain we shall know.*

> *A rainbow in the morn put your hook in the corn;*
> *A rainbow at eve, put your hand in the sheave.*
>   (Old nursery rhyme)

The cricket has been known for centuries as "the poor man's thermometer." (*See* CRICKETS) If you count the number of chirps within fifteen seconds, then add the number thirty-seven, you'll get the temperature in Fahrenheit degrees.

WEDDING CAKE

See WEDDING CUSTOMS

WEDDING CUSTOMS

The state of holy wedlock—how many times have you heard that expression? Wed is an old Anglo-Saxon word meaning to assign property to the bride's father as payment; lock simply means a pledge. Wedlock then is the promise to pay for the bride. What's so holy about that?

The first marriage was the kind between a caveman and the woman he chose. Most likely he'd sneak into her encampment, steal her, and hide her away in a cave until things calmed down again.

Many of our wedding customs are grounded in those early times. Some have real symbolism, others are based on a tradition whose meaning has died long ago. Here is a brief look at some of the traditions we keep alive today.

The *engagement ring*: A ring of any kind represents a pledge, and so when early Teutonic couples became engaged or betrothed, the man placed a ring on the right hand of his intended. The ring was a sign that the woman was off limits to other knights passing through the area.

June weddings: "Prosperity to the man and happiness to the maid when married in June," was an ancient Roman proverb. The Romans named June for the goddess Juno, the deity of women, and they believed that she blessed marriages that took place in her month. June is the favored month for weddings in the Western world more than in the East.

Brides: In old English the word bride came from a name for cook; that should make everything clear. *Grooms*: This was derived from male child; and *bridegroom* should mean a male cook, but it doesn't. It comes from German and means what it appears to mean—the person marrying the bride.

Bridesmaids and ushers: These come from the old Roman law that required ten witnesses to outwit the evil spirits who usually attended happy functions. The bridesmaids and ushers were dressed like the bride and groom so that the Devil wouldn't know who was getting married. Later, ushers, or groomsmen, were very useful to the bridegroom. They stood watch during the honeymoon period.

During the Middle Ages, man often reverted to the more primitive days of his caveman ancestors and simply kidnapped a woman and married her. The irate members of her family would come riding after her, but once the marriage had been consummated, nobody wanted her back. The ushers stood guard during the honeymoon. (*See* HONEYMOONS)

The accoutrements of the wedding ceremony, such as the *veil*, the *ring*, and the *white gown*, are all rooted in solid superstition. The wedding veil, for instance, probably comes from the Greeks and Romans. It is a vestige of the bridal canopy, which was constructed to keep the evil eye away from the wedding festivities. It is also an early Eastern custom that the bride should never be seen by the groom before the marriage as a sign of submission to her family. The raising of the veil is a symbol of freedom from parental control.

The *wedding ring* seals the bargain. A bride was considered property and the ring, in some societies, was a token of purchase. "With this ring" takes on a different meaning when viewed that way, doesn't it? The wedding ring is placed on the third finger of the left hand because it was believed that a love vein ran directly from the heart through that finger. If the ring was removed the love would escape from the heart.

> *Married when the year is new,*
> *He'll be loving, kind and true.*
> *When February birds do mate*
> *You wed nor dread your fate.*
> *If you wed when March winds blow*
> *Joy and sorrow both you'll know.*
> *Marry in April when you can*
> *Joy for maiden and the man.*
> *Marry in the month of May*
> *And you'll surely rue the day.*
> *Marry when June roses grow*
> *Over land and sea you'll go.*
> *Those who in July do wed*

Must labor for their daily bread.
Whoever wed in August be,
Many a change is sure to see.
Marry in September's shine,
Your living will be rich and fine.
If in October you do marry
Love will come, but riches tarry.
If you wed in bleak November
Only joys will come, remember
When December's snows fall fast,
Marry and true love will last.
                    (Old English rhyme)

The *bridal bouquet* always has knots at the end of its ribbons. They represent good wishes and are also known as lover's knots, symbolic of oneness and unity. Throwing the bouquet is a fairly modern tradition: the one who catches it is sure to be the next to marry.

Orange blossoms are frequently found in the bridal bouquet. The custom goes back to the Saracens. The orange blossoms stand for chastity and purity. The orange blossom tree is an evergreen, which represents everlasting love, and is therefore the ideal symbol for a wedding.

The white gown of the bride was initially a symbol of joy. It dates at least to the Greeks, who sometimes even painted their bodies white before a marriage ceremony. The meaning of white has changed somewhat and now is purity and chastity more than joy.

"Something old, something new, something borrowed, something blue" is a rhyme that comes to us from merry old England. The something old of tradition was an old garter from a happily married woman. The notion of sympathetic magic is at work here. If the garter came from a happily married woman, it could pass along her happiness to the new couple. Something borrowed was, in olden times, a piece of gold representing the sun, the source of all life. Something blue was a compliment to the moon, the traditional protector of all women. Something new was anything at all, usually the wedding gown.

The *bridal kiss* is the groom sealing his sacred pledge. There is a tradition that it is lucky if the bride cries at about this time during the ceremony. If she doesn't cry, there will be tears throughout the marriage.

The tradition of *breaking a glass* is found in Jewish wedding ceremonies and is also important to the Hindus. The sound of the breaking glass was believed to scare the evil spirits away. It also symbolized the consummation of the marriage: the man's virility, and the woman's hyman being broken. A third interpretation is that it symbolized the destruction of the temple in Jerusalem reminding the participants how fleeting happiness can be.

When the ceremony is over it's time for the *wedding feast*, an ancient custom which is probably as old as weddings themselves. The ancients observed what they called "eating together."

At the feast there is always a *wedding cake*, which first became popular with the Romans, who broke a cake made of meal over the bride's head for luck. Then all the guests would sprinkle the crumbs from the cake over their own heads for luck. This cake sprinkling was meant to represent a wish that the newlyweds would have good things throughout their married lives. When today's bride cuts the first slice of the cake she is aided by her new husband so that he can share in the good luck. There is also an old custom of the bride putting a piece of the wedding cake under her bridal bed as a symbol of faithfulness.

The feasting is now over, and the wedding couple is ready to leave. Someone begins *throwing rice*, a symbol of fertility, prosperity, and health, and a way of chasing the evil spirits away from the couple. The Orientals began this custom, and the Romans changed it to suit their own culture. They threw nuts (a little more dangerous sometimes, but the meaning was the same) and later European cultures threw confetti (much safer and cheaper).

Then someone ties the *old shoes* to the fender of the bridal car. This custom comes from a time when the father of the bride gave the woman's old shoes to the husband as a symbol that he was now responsible for her.

The newlyweds are on their way to their *honeymoon*, a word, probably invented by the Teutons, referring to the mead mixed with honey that couples drank during the first month of marriage. (*See* HONEYMOONS)

Finally, the wedding is over, the honeymoon has been a sheer delight, and the *new husband carries his bride over the threshold*, which comes from the times when a man stole his bride away and also prevents the bride from tripping or using the wrong foot (the left foot would be the wrong foot) when stepping over the threshold of her new home. It is believed to be a sign of very bad luck for her to do either. (*See* RIGHT SIDE OF BED).

WEDDING FEAST

See WEDDING CUSTOMS

WEDDING RING

See WEDDING CUSTOMS

WEDDING VEIL

See WEDDING CUSTOMS

WEREWOLF

This was a very popular medieval superstition. The werewolf was a person turned into a wolf through an enchantment or a charm; or a person who could turn himself (or herself) into a wolf. The ways of the werewolf were frightening to those who knew about them. Werewolves roamed the countryside at night, eating babies and other human's flesh; or if they were very hungry, digging up corpses. Their skin was virtually weaponproof, unless the weapon had been specially blessed.

In the Middle Ages, the belief in werewolves was so common that a convention of theologians was called in the fifteenth century; and after careful discussion, they solemnly decreed that werewolves really existed.

The notion originated in early Greco-Roman times, and Ovid wrote of a werewolf at the beginning of the first century.

The most famous modern werewolf is probably in Robert Louis Stevenson's *Strange Case of Dr. Jekyll and Mr. Hyde*, in which the respectable Dr. Jekyll became the evil, werewolflike Mr. Hyde.

WHISTLING

Whistling in the house invites the Devil.
If little girls whistle, they'll grow beards.
Whistling aboard ship will raise a storm
Never whistle in the dressing room of a theater. (*See* THE-
ATRICAL FEARS)
Reporters who whistle in editorial rooms or miners who whistle underground are asking for trouble.

It has been said that a woman whistled while the nails were forged for the cross, and so every time a woman whistles, the Virgin Mary's heart bleeds.

Ancient man was afraid to whistle. He thought that if you whistled, the Devil would answer. The logic behind this belief was that the Devil or evil spirits were usually thought to be responsible for all sounds that man couldn't account for, such as whistling wind through the trees and the sounds of the wind before a storm.

WHITE

See also CHARTS, Colors
　　　　WEDDING CUSTOMS
　　　　WHITE ELEPHANT
　　　　WHITE HORSE

White is the symbol of purity, simplicity, candor, innocence, truth, and hope. It was the color of the ancient clergy and of the druids. The sacrifices made to the great god Jupiter were offered while dressed in white. At Caesar's death, white was proclaimed the national mourning color. The Magi were thought to have worn white when delivering their gifts to Christ.

The Chinese still wear white for mourning. (*See* DEATH CUSTOMS)

WHITE ELEPHANT

In today's usage, a white elephant is something that's very expensive to maintain and from which no one profits. It all started in Siam (today's Thailand), where white elephants were so rare they were immediately given to the king and placed under his protection. They were revered and so could not be made to work for their upkeep. There is a story that when a nobleman did something to displease the king, he was given a white elephant by the ruler, who then waited for the expense of keeping this hungry creature to ruin the nobleman. It didn't take very long.

When P. T. Barnum bought a white elephant to appear as an attraction in his circus, it cost him 200,000 dollars just to get it to New York—now there's a white elephant for you.

WHITE GOWN

See WEDDING CUSTOMS

WHITE HORSE

Everybody knows the good guy rides a white horse; or do they?

A white horse was the symbol for purity and was thought to be able to warn of danger.

When a white horse passes, spit over your little finger for good luck and lick one thumb and stamp it into the palm of the other hand (stamping out the Devil) to avoid bad luck. At the same time, say, "Criss cross, white hoss, money for the week's done."

In some regions of England, particularly around the Midlands and in the South, the white horse is associated with murder. It seems the Saxons's banner showed a white horse, and after a bloody war in which the Saxons conquered the area, the white horse banner could be seen everywhere. When the natives saw a Saxon white horse go by they would spit over their left shoulders to banish the evil spirits created by the Saxons's presence. Many people still spit over their shoulders at the sight of a white horse.

There's an old wives' tale that white horses live longer than dark ones. Consequently, many people consider the white horse a living amulet against an early death.

WIDOW'S PEAK

Some people are born with the lovely V-shaped hairline that characterizes the widow's peak. Others try to cultivate one. Some think it's a sign of intelligence and long life; others think it's merely pretty.

There is an important superstition about the widow's peak you women ought to know before you create your own versions. It says that you will lose your first husband young and marry again soon. This goes back to 1498, when Anne of Brittany mourned the death of her husband Charles VIII. Anne married the French king Louis XII very soon after, so don't worry about her. Hat designers of the time created a new black V-shaped bonnet for Anne (who was the first for centuries to wear black for mourning) that suggested the V-shaped hairline and became known as the widow's peak.

WINE

Even back in the first century A.D., "in wine there is truth" was a common proverb. The ancients, who loved wine, believed that it contained spirits. When wine was drunk the spirits of the wine became active, and as we all know, spirits never lie. They therefore believed that spilling wine was a warning by the spirits that bad luck was on the way. The countercharm to that was to place some of the wine behind the ears with the middle finger of the right hand.

There is a superstition that spilling champagne is a bad omen. Sparkling wine was actually invented by accident when some monks put a cork in their wine bottles instead of the usual stopper. The wine mixed with the cork, creating the carbonic acid needed for carbonation. The Church believed that the carbonation was an evil spirit and champagne was outlawed for quite some time, although it never really disappeared from the market.

WISHBONES

If you believe your wish will come true when you win the break in a wishbone contest, then you're following in the footsteps of civilizations dating back to the Etruscans, 322 B.C.

Before digital clocks and morning disc jockeys, man waited for the cock to crow; and when he wanted an egg he waited for the hen to announce the coming of her product. This made the two animals mystical in that they could tell the future. They were the origins of the hen oracles.

To receive an answer to an important question from these oracles a man would draw a circle on the ground and divide it into the twenty-four letters of the alphabet. Grains of corn were placed in each section, and the cock or hen was led into the circle and then set free. It was believed that the fowl would spell out words or symbols by picking up kernels of corn from the different sections. For example, the first letter of a future husband's name would be the first kernel of corn picked. After writing the message, the fowl was sacrificed to a special deity and its collarbone was hung out to dry.

The person seeking answers made a wish on the bone. Then two other people got a chance to make a wish by snapping the dried bone in the same fashion we do, each one pulling one end. The person with the larger end of the bone was the one who got the wish. This was known as a lucky break.

The Romans picked up the wishbone habit and brought it with them when they conquered England. That's how we got it.

WISHFUL THINKING

If a man could have half his wishes
he would double his troubles.
(Benjamin Franklin,
Poor Richard's Almanack)

As we have seen, man has always believed in the concept of like makes like and it is at the heart of many superstitions. Wishful thinking is an extension of that belief. In early times man thought that he would have all his wishes answered if he made a wish while looking at or touching something that resembled the riches he prayed for; if only that were true.

WISHING ON A COIN

See WISHING WELLS

WISHING WELLS

You probably wouldn't have to wish for wealth if you still had all the coins you've tossed into wishing wells. Still you continue to throw coins in, make a wish, and wait for the results.

In the old days, the sea gods demanded tributes. The Greeks, for instance, tossed coins into their wells in the hope that they wouldn't run dry; a little bribe, you might say.

The tradition is that if you throw a coin into a well or a fountain, wait for the water to clear enough to see your own reflection, and then make your wish, the sea gods will make your wish come true. Some think it's the water spirits who accomplish this magic.

Niagara Falls, it is said, yields up thousands of dollars each year.

WISH ON A STAR

Star light, star bright
Here's the wish I wish tonight.
I wish I may, I wish I might
Have the wish I wish tonight.
                    (Anonymous)

People make wishes on anything new: the first star, a new moon, the first load of hay harvested, the first robin redbreast, and other firsts. There is a special magic in firsts.

Most people believe that wishes can come true if all the circumstances are right; most notably, that you keep the wish to yourself, never telling it to a soul. Of course we all know if you want something badly enough you'll probably get it, because you'll do everything you have to do to accomplish it. Then you'll go and pay tribute to some supernatural source for your success

One very popular superstition about wishing involves the moment when two people say the same word at the same time. Their wishes will come true if they link right pinkies and take turns saying:

Needles
Pins
Triplets
Twins.
When we marry
Our trouble begins.
What goes up a chimney?
Smoke
What comes down a chimney?
Santa Claus.

Then say together:

May your wish and my wish never be broken.

WITCHES AND WARLOCKS

Thou shalt not suffer a witch to live.
(The Book of Exodus)

How now, you secret, black and midnight hags!
(Shakespeare, *Macbeth*)

Those midnight hags that Shakespeare wrote of—the most famous witches in history—were created many hundreds of years before the famous playwright.

Witches were devised by pagan leaders to answer the questions evil happenings pose. The witches were originally envisioned as women who had made a pact with the Devil. Men were often sorcerers and wizards, and later in history, warlocks. Both witches and sorcerers practiced what was called black magic, which was defined as a supernatural power.

In some civilizations the medicine man and the wise old women performed the same function, that of explaining evil. It wasn't until the churches of organized religion defined good and evil that the witches of older times became truly evil, malignant creatures. It wasn't until the Middle Ages that witches and sorcerers were rooted out and burned at the stake.

The first witch in history may have been Homer's Circe, who was depicted as having the ability to cast spells on men and turn them into animals. Circe was believed to be very beautiful, and once a man heard her song he fell under her spell. Her image became corrupted through the centuries. A witch was then believed to be an ugly hag who rode broomsticks and cast spells by the light of the moon.

As the stories grew, so did the powers of the witch. She could change her form and become a cat or a rabbit. She was responsible for dead babies, sick cows, bad crops—you name it, she did it. Witches could cast spells with poisons, potions, chants and charms, or she could stick dolls with pins, as in voodoo. Witches remain an important part of many religions and there are many people today who claim to have the powers of a witch, although most of these say they are good witches who practice white magic.

If you run into a witch you will recognize her by:

> eyebrows that grow together
> birthmarks (particularly under the arm)
> red hair
> the evil eye

You'll also notice that a witch can't stand the presence of iron; has no reflection in a mirror (because she has no soul); is able to recite the Lord's prayer backward; can turn herself into birds except a robin redbreast (*See* ROBIN REDBREAST); and can't cry.

One infallible test for a witch, popular in the Middle Ages, was called the trial by water. If a suspected witch was thrown into the water and surfaced, she was guilty and was allowed to drown. If the person drowned without surfacing she was presumed innocent, but of course, by then it didn't matter for her.

WOMAN SCORNED

This is purely a literary reference, and I've included it in this book of superstitions because many think it has a base in the world of quasi fact.

> *Heaven has no rage like love to hatred turned,*
> *Nor hell a fury like a woman scorned.*
> (Congreve, *The Mourning Bride*)

> We shall find no fiend in hell
> Can match the fury of a
> Disappointed woman,
> Scorned, slighted, dismissed
> Without a parting pang.
> (Colley Cibber,
> *Love's Last Shift*, IV:1)

It's a bum rap!

WORTH HIS WEIGHT IN GOLD

See BIRTHDAYS

YANKEE DOODLE

As a British Army doctor sat watching the American troops, he doodled with words and came up with a ditty that made fun of the "homely clad colonials." Ironically "Yankee Doodle" became America's first patriotic song.

The words of Dr. Richard Shuckburg's poem were set to a traditional English folksong, or, says the folklorist Tristram Coffin, a Dutch farm song. The song was picked up by the rebels and sung with great gusto by the troops at the surrender of General Cornwallis at Yorktown.

The only confusing part of the song is "stuck a feather in his cap, and called it macaroni." Americans had little idea what it meant, but they sang it anyway. Actually, it referred to the Macaroni Club, popular in London at the time, which was a club of fops and over-dressed young men who wanted to bring the lushness of Continental fashions to England.

> *Yankee Doodle went to London*
> *riding on a pony,*
> *He stuck a feather in his cap*
> *and called it Macaroni.*

Yankee Doodle keep it up,
Yankee Doodle Dandy;
Mind the music and the step
and with the girls be handy.

Father and I went down to camp,
Along with Captain Goodin'
And there we saw the men and boys
As thick as hasty puddin'.
(Edward Bangs, c. 1775)

YAWNING

There is only one yawn in the world,
and it goes from person to person.
(Anonymous)

The people of the Middle Ages believed the Devil entered your mouth through a yawn; and so it was very important either to make the sign of the cross over your mouth when you yawned or to cover your mouth.

Some early civilizations thought they'd lose their breath, never get it back, and die, so they covered their yawns, too. Some ancients believed that yawning was a sign of danger and anyone who caught the yawn was in that danger.

The Hindus are afraid of a yawn, and they snap their fingers three times to dispel the danger. In Finland, it is said that yawning horses mean rain. Hippocrates believed that intense yawning indicated the onset of a fever.

Yawning does seem to be contagious. It's actually an oxygen deficiency and if you're in a room with little oxygen it will probably not be long before several people in the room start yawning.

My particular favorite about yawning is that it is supposed to be a silent shout for help.

YELLOW

See also CHARTS, Colors
　　　THEATRICAL FEARS

> *all looks yellow to the jaundic'd eye.*
> (Pope, *An Essay on Criticism II*)

Yellow is the color of jealousy, inconstancy, and even treachery. In France, the doors of traitors were streaked with yellow paint.

Judas is often pictured in yellow. In some countries, during ancient times, Jews were made to wear yellow to indicate their treachery in betraying Christ. The infamous star Jews were forced to wear by Nazis was yellow.

Yellow is also the color of cowards. "He has a yellow streak" means he's scared.

In Spain, executioners sometimes wore yellow.

YIN AND YANG

*The dots of opposite color on each side represent
the knowledge that nothing is all black or all white*

Yin and yang together form the meaning of the universe in ancient Chinese philosophy. This presents two forces that are in constant opposition but form a perfect whole.

Yin, the black side of the circle, represents the female, earthly power in the universe. This is the negative, dark side, containing shadows and water. Yang, the white side of the circle, is the male, active, positive, and powerful side, representing the heavenly powers in the universe, the light, the sun, and the warmth. Together, yin, coolness of shade, and yang, warmth of the sun, make up life on earth.

The concept of yin and yang was first developed during the Chou dynasty (c. 1122–221 B.C) and later became part of Confucianism. It is, to some degree, still part of Chinese philosophy. The symbol is often seen in oriental countries.

ZODIAC

The word zodiac comes from a Latin word for animal or living being and the Greek word for life. The zodiac is an imaginary belt drawn through the sky dividing it into twelve constellations, which corresponded with the Greek animal constellations. The idea of the zodiac and its believers go back about four thousand years.

Everyone has a zodiacal sign, determined by when he or she was born. Many believe that the influence of the stars upon birth is so strong that a person's character and personality are formed by the sign under which he was born.

The twelve signs of the zodiac have been extremely popular

amulets for centuries. (*See* AMULETS) To determine which sign
you should carry, consult the following chart:

Sign	*Birthday*
ARIES, *The Ram*	March 21–April 20
TAURUS, *The Bull*	April 21–May 20
GEMINI, *The Twins*	May 21–June 20
CANCER, *The Crab*	June 21–July 22
LEO, *The Lion*	July 23–August 22
VIRGO, *The Virgin*	August 23–September 22
LIBRA, *The Balance*	September 23–October 22
SCORPIO, *The Scorpion*	October 23–November 22
SAGGITTARIUS, *The Archer*	November 23–December 21
CAPRICORN, *The Goat*	December 22–January 19
AQUARIUS, *The Water Bearer*	January 20–February 18
PISCES, *The Fish*	February 19–March 20

APPENDIX

BODY PARTS GOVERNED BY ZODIAC SIGNS

CAPRICORN	(December 22–January 19)	Knees and circulation
AQUARIUS	(January 20–February 18)	Back and legs
PISCES	(February 19–March 20)	Feet
ARIES	(March 21–April 20)	Head
TAURUS	(April 21–May 20)	Throat
GEMINI	(May 21–June 20)	Arms, chest, and lungs
CANCER	(June 21–July 22)	Stomach and breast
LEO	(July 23–August 22)	Heart and the small of the back
VIRGO	(August 23–September 22)	Intestines
LIBRA	(September 23–October 22)	Liver and kidneys
SCORPIO	(October 23–November 22)	Backside and reproductive organs
SAGITTARIUS	(November 23–December 21)	Legs, hips, and thighs

BIRTHSTONES

JANUARY
Capricorn
Garnet for Fidelity. Believed to repel flying insects, and to help the wearer be firm and steadfast.

FEBRUARY
Aquarius
Amethyst for Sincerity. Believed to protect against drunkenness and falling in love foolishly, and to encourage calmness in the wearer.

MARCH
Pisces
Aquamarine for Courage and Truth. Understood to bring wisdom, success, and popularity to those who wear it.

APRIL
Aries
Diamond for Innocence. This stone will bring victory to its wearer.

MAY
Taurus
Emerald for Happiness. It will insure a life of love and success, and protect against all eye diseases.

JUNE *Gemini*	Pearl for Long Life. This stone brings health, wealth, and good luck to the wearer.
JULY *Cancer*	Ruby for Peace of Mind. Believed to heal wounds, prevent stomachaches and bring love to its wearer.
AUGUST *Leo*	Sardonyx (a form of onyx) for Happiness. The wearer will have a happy marriage, contentment, and personal satisfaction.
SEPTEMBER *Virgo*	Sapphire for Wisdom. As a charm, this stone is believed to relieve headaches, protect the wearer from the evil eye, and clear the head of the wearer to allow wise thinking.
OCTOBER *Libra*	Opal for Hope. The wearer of this stone will receive good luck.
NOVEMBER *Scorpio*	Topaz for Loyalty. Believed to guard the wearer against calamity; and to insure faithful friendships.
DECEMBER *Sagittarius*	Turquoise for Success. This stone is supposed to protect wearers against accidents, and to make them prosperous.

COLORS

Colors speak all languages.
(Addison, in *The Spector*, 1712)

BLACK	Black, the color of pitch, was used to cover mummies. For the ancients, it was a symbol of resurrection and rebirth. In more modern times, it has come to mean death and mourning. (*See* BLACK)
BLUE	Wear blue as protection against witches and the malice of the evil eye. Blue stands for truth and creative power. Blue is the color of the heavens and is therefore one of the luckiest colors.

GREEN	Green is an unlucky color because it is the color of the small folks (*See* SMALL FOLKS), and you wouldn't want to anger the gnomes and leprechauns. It's bad luck to wear green onstage or at a Christening. It is especially unlucky for lovers. Green is the symbol of the resurrection because plants are green.
GOLD	Gold was the color of the gods in the ancient world, and largely because of the value of gold ore, it has remained a sacred color.
ORANGE	The word for orange comes from Sanskrit. It was the color of the early Church, symbol of the fruits of the earth.
RED	Red has always been considered an evil color, ever since its association with the Egyptian god Set, an evil and unlucky god. Men with red beards were considered evil. Red objects became popular amulets and talismans because it is believed that witches and the Devil are afraid of red. (*See* AMULETS; RED RIBBONS)
WHITE	White stands for joy, purity, and innocence. (*See* WHITE)
YELLOW	Yellow is an unlucky color. Actors who played the Devil in medieval plays wore yellow. In many areas Jews were forced to wear yellow as a symbol of the betrayal of Christ. Yellow is for jealousy. (*See* YELLOW)

Green's forsaken
Yellow's foresworn
Blue's the color
That shall be worn.

Blue is true
Yellow's jealous
Green's forsaken
White is love
And black is death.

EDIBLE PLANTS AND THEIR MEANINGS

ALMOND	Stupid, Indiscreet, and Thoughtless
CABBAGE	For Profit
CHICORY	Frugality
CORN	Riches
CRANBERRY	Cure for Headaches
CUCUMBER	Criticism
CURRANTS	Pleases Everyone
ENDIVE	Frugality
FIGS	Arguments and Longevity
GOOSEBERRY	Anticipation
LETTUCE	Coldhearted
MUSHROOM	Suspicion
OLIVE	Peace
PEACH	You're Terrific
PEAR	Affection
PEPPERMINT	Warm and Cordial
PINEAPPLE	You're Perfect
POMEGRANATE	Foolishness
POTATO	Benevolent
PUMPKIN	Bulkiness
QUINCE	Temptation
RASPBERRY	Remorse
RHUBARB	Advice
SPEARMINT	Warm Sentiments
STRAWBERRY	Perfect, Excellent
TURNIP	Charity
WALNUT	Intellectual
WATERMELON	Chunky
WHEAT	Prosperity
WILD GRAPES	Charity

FLOWERS
*and the months to which they are dedicated**

See also CHARTS, Language of Flowers

JANUARY	Carnations and Snowdrops
FEBRUARY	Violets and Primroses
MARCH	Daffodils and Jonquils
APRIL	Daisies and Sweet Peas
MAY	Lilies of the Valley and Hawthorn
JUNE	Roses and Honeysuckle
JULY	Water Lilies and Larkspur
AUGUST	Gladiolus and Poppies
SEPTEMBER	Morning Glories and Asters
OCTOBER	Calendula and Cosmos
NOVEMBER	Chrysanthemums
DECEMBER	Narcissus and Holly

*This is to help give the appropriate flowers to people as dictated by the months in which they were born. The above list indicates which flower is lucky to which month.

GREEK LANGUAGE OF THE MOLE

See BIRTHMARKS

IF THE MOLE IS:	IT MEANS:
Above the right eye	Wealth and a happy marriage
Above the left eye	Healthy interest in the opposite sex, which would bring joy
Temple	Happiness in love
Nose	Success in business
Chin	Lucky with friends
Cheek	Happiness without fame or fortune
Ear	Contented nature
Arms	Happy nature

Shoulders	Able to face problems with courage
Hands	Practical nature, able to care for yourself
Legs	Strong-willed
Neck	Patience

HERBS AND SENTIMENTS

ALLSPICE	Compassion
BASIL	Hatred
BAY LEAF	I change, but only in death
CHERVIL	Sincerity
CLOVES	Dignity
CORIANDER	Hidden virtues
FENNEL	Brute force
LAUREL (GROUND)	Perseverance
MARJORAM	Blushes
MINT	Virtue
MUSTARD SEED	Indifference
MYRRH	Gladness
PARSLEY	Feasting
ROSEMARY	Remembrance
SAFFRON	Don't overdo
SAGE	Domestic virtues
SORREL	Parental affection
SWEET BASIL	Good wishes
THYME	Activity

HOLIDAYS

NEW YEAR'S DAY	January 1 (*See* NEW YEAR'S DAY)
MARTIN LUTHER KING DAY	January 15
CHINESE NEW YEAR	Sometime between January 21 and February 19 depending on Chinese calendar
GROUNDHOG DAY (Candlemas Day)	February 2 (*See* GROUNDHOG DAY)
MARDI GRAS	Tuesday before Ash Wednesday
SAINT VALENTINE'S DAY	February 14 (*See* VALENTINE)
SAINT PATRICK'S DAY	March 17 (*See* SHAMROCKS)
GOOD FRIDAY	Friday before Easter
APRIL FOOLS' DAY	April 1 (*See* APRIL FOOLS' DAY)
EASTER	Sometime between March 22 and April 30; Sunday after the first full moon after the vernal equinox (*See* EASTER; EASTER EGGS)
MOTHER'S DAY	May 10 (*See* MOTHER'S DAY)
ARMED FORCES DAY	Third Saturday in May
FATHER'S DAY	Third Saturday in June
INDEPENDENCE DAY	July 4
ROSH HASHANAH AND YOM KIPPUR	Sometime between September and October determined by the Jewish calendar
COLUMBUS DAY	October 12
HALLOWE'EN	October 31 (*See* HALLOWE'EN)
VETERAN'S DAY	November 11
THANKSGIVING	Fourth Thursday in November (*See* THANKSGIVING)
HANUKKAH	Sometime between November and December determined by the Jewish calendar
CHRISTMAS DAY	December 25 (*See* CHRISTMAS)
NEW YEAR'S EVE	December 31 (*See* NEW YEAR'S DAY)

MONTHS

JANUARY The old Welsh proverb that says, "a warm January; a cold May," has haunted farmers for centuries. Another proverb, popular among farmers, is "A mild January means bad luck for both man and beast." January was named after the Roman god Janus, keeper of the gates; a two-headed creature, Janus had the ability to see both the past and the future.

FEBRUARY The Italians say, "February, the shortest month in the year, is also the worst." February was the Roman month of purification. It was the shortest month because Augustus Caesar took a day from February and added it to August to make that month (which had been named after him) longer than July (which had been named for Julius Caesar.)

MARCH "Beware the ides of March" was Shakespeare's idea (in *Julius Caesar*). The month of March had been named after Mars, the God of War. It has been said that to marry in March when the winds blow means you'll experience both joy and sorrow in your wedded life. March used to hold New Year's Day, which was celebrated on March 25.

APRIL "April's in her eyes; it is love's Spring," wrote Shakespeare (in *Antony and Cleopatra*, III:2). The month of April was probably named for the goddess Aphrodite, the Greek goddess of love. It marks the arrival of Spring and is a favorite among poets.

MAY

"The vulgar say that it is unlucky to marry in May," said Ovid (*Fasti* 5) during the opening days of the first century. This idea probably got started because the Romans honored the dead in the month of May; yet, it is a month dedicated to love. The remaining days of the month are a time for the revival of crops, flowers, and of life in general. The month may have been named for Maia, daughter of Atlas, god of growth.

JUNE

And what is so rare as a day in June?
Then, if ever, come perfect days.
(Lowell, *The Vision of Sir Launfal*, I, 1848)

As everyone knows, June is the month for marriages, probably because the month was named for Juno, wife of Jupiter and goddess of women, marriages, and childbirth. On June 1, Romans honored Juno, and ever since the month has been the luckiest to be married in.

JULY

July was named in honor of Julius Caesar in 44 B.C. It may not have been such an honor after all, since the dog days happen during July. (*See* DOG DAYS)

Hot July brings cooling showers,
Apricots and gillyflowers.
(Sara Colridge, *Pretty Lessons in Verse*, 1834)

AUGUST

Since Julius took July, his successor, Augustus Caesar, took August (seems only fair, doesn't it?). The month marked the beginning of harvest.

If the twenty-fourth of August be fair and clear,
Then hope for a prosperous Autumn that year.
(John Ray, *English Proverbs*, 1670)

SEPTEMBER   September was originally the seventh month of the Roman year and was named after the number seven. It was a time to finish harvesting and to celebrate the results.

The golden rod is yellow
The corn is turning brown
The trees in apple orchards
With fruit are bending down...
By all these lovely tokens
September days are here,
With summer's best of weather
And autumn's best of cheer.
(Helen Hunt Jackson, *September*)

OCTOBER   The month of October was named for the word eight, because it was the Romans' eighth month on the calendar. October means (though not literally) autumn. It is the last gasp before the winter winds set in and the snows start to fall.

October is nature's funeral month... The month of departure is more beautiful than the month of coming... Every green thing loves to die in bright colors.
(Beecher, *Proverbs from Plymouth Pulpit*, 1870)

NOVEMBER   November is Latin for ninth... and has been called "the month of blue devil and suicides." In the British Isles, it was once believed that November cast an evil spell over men's minds because of its monotonous, dreary days. A French novelist is supposed to have written, in 1712, "The gloomy month of November, when the people of England hang and drown themselves."

DECEMBER   December, from the Latin for tenth, was dedicated to Saturn, god of seed sowing. The Saxons honored Thor, god of thunder on December 21, which they called Giul. That became yule. When the Saxons converted to Christianity, they called the month Heiligh-monath, meaning holy month. Shakespeare saw December from a different perspective:

> *When we shall hear*
> *The rain and wind beat dark December.*
> *(Cymbeline*, III:3)

MOST POPULAR SUPERSTITIONS

- Wishing on a wishbone
- Believing in the power of the horseshoe
- Carrying a rabbit's foot
- Looking for a four-leaf clover
- Seven years' bad luck from a broken mirror
- Getting out of bed on the right side
- Bad luck to walk under a ladder
- Belief in the power of Friday the thirteenth
- Looking at the new moon over your right shoulder for luck
- Consider seven a lucky number
- Won't light three cigarettes on one match
- Never invite thirteen to dinner
- Believe in the implications of spilled salt
- Never open an umbrella indoors
- Make a wish on a falling star or the first star of the night
- The wearing of amulets or talismans for luck
- Find a pin, pick it up, all day you'll have good luck
- Saying "God Bless You" to someone who sneezes

NAMES

Female

ALICE	Truth
AMY	Beloved
ANN	Full of grace, mercy, and prayer
APRIL	To open
ARLENE	A pledge
AUDREY	Strong and noble
BARBARA	Mysterious stranger
BEATRICE	She brings joy
BEVERLY	Ambitious
BRENDA	Fiery
CANDICE	Pure
CAROL	Joyous song
CAROLINE	One who is strong
COLETTE	Victorious
CYNTHIA	Moon goddess
DAISY	The day's eve
DARLENE	Dearly beloved
DOROTHY	The bee
DIANA	Pure goddess of the moon
ELAINE (Eleanor)	Light
ELIZABETH	Consecrated to God
EMILY	Industrious
ENID	Purity of soul
EVE	Life or living
FLORENCE	To flower or bloom
FRANCES	Free
GABRIELLE	Woman of God
GERALDINE	Ruler with a spear
GLORIA	The glorious
GRACE	The graceful
GWEN	White-browed
HARRIET	Mistress of the home
HELEN	Light
HILARY	Cheerful friend

HOLLY	Good luck
IDA	Happy
IRENE	Peace
ISABEL	Consecrated to God
JACQUELINE	The supplanter
JANE	God's gracious gift
JESSICA	Rice; grace of God
JOSEPHINE	She shall add
JUDITH	Admired, praised
JULIA	Youthful
KATHERINE	Pure
KIM	Noble or glorious leader
LAURA	The laurel
LEE	Meadow
LESLEY	From the gray fort
LILLIAN	A lily
LINDA	Beautiful
LOUISE	Battle maiden
LUCY	Light
LYNN	Life
MADELINE	Tower of strength
MARCIA	Of Mars
MARGARET	A pearl
MARTHA	The lady
MARY	Bitter
MELANIE	Darkness
MELISSA	Honeybee
NANCY	Full of grace
NAOMI	Sweet
NATALIE	Child of Christmas
NICOLE	Victory of the people
ORIANA	Girl of the white skin
PATRICIA	Wellborn
PAULA	Little
PHYLLIS	A green bough
PIA	Devout
POLLY	Bitter
PRISCILLA	Of ancient lineage

RACHEL	Trembling child
RENEE	Reborn
RHODA	A garland of roses
RITA	A pearl
ROSALIND	Fair rose
RUTH	Beautiful friend
SAMANTHA	Lovely flower
SARAH	Princess
SHARON	From the fertile plain
SHEILA	Musical
SOPHIA	Wisdom
STEPHANIE	Crown or garland
SUSAN	A lily
SYBIL	The prophetess
TALLULAH	Vivacious
TERESA	The harvester
TIFFANY	Manifestation of God
ULLA	Dearest of all God's burdens
VALENTINA	Vigorous and strong
VANESSA	The butterfly
VERONICA	True image
VICTORIA	Victorious
VIRGINIA	Maidenly, pure
WENDY	White-browed
YVONNE	The archer
ZOE	Life

Male

AARON	Light, high mountain
ADAM	Man of earth
ALAN	Harmony
ALEXANDER	Protector of me
ANDREW	Manly
ANTHONY	Of inestimable worth
ARTHUR	Strong as a rock
BARNABY	Son of consolation
BENJAMIN	Son of my right hand
BRIAN	Strong, powerful

CALVIN	Bald
CASEY	Valorous
CHARLES	Man
CHRISTOPHER	Christ bearer
CLARK	Scholarly
DANIEL	The Lord is judge
DAVID	Beloved
DENNIS	Lover of fine wines
DONALD	Ruler of the world
DOUGLAS	From the black stream
EDWARD	Prosperous guardian
ERIC	Kingly
FRANCIS	Free
FRANKLIN	A free man
GARY	Mighty spear
GEORGE	Farmer
GERALD	Mighty spearman
GILBERT	Bright pledge
GORDON	From the cornered hill
GREGORY	Vigilant
HENRY	Home ruler
HOWARD	Chief guardian
HUGH	Intelligence
IRA	Watcher
IRWIN	Sea friend
ISRAEL	The Lord's soldier
JAMES	The supplanter
JAY	Crow; lively
JEFFREY	Exalted by God
JOEL	Jehovah is God
JOHN	God's gracious gift
JONATHAN	Gift of the Lord
JOSEPH	He shall add
JOSIAH	He is healed by the Lord
JUSTIN	The just
KENNETH	Handsome
KEVIN	Kind, gentle
LANCE	Spear

LAWRENCE	Laurel
LEE	Meadow
LEWIS	Renowned for battle
LLOYD	Gray or dark
MARK	Warrior
MARTIN	Warrior
MATTHEW	God's gift
MICHAEL	God-like
MORGAN	From the sea
MURRAY	Sailor
NATHANIEL	Gift of God
NICHOLAS	Victory of the people
NORMAN	Man of the north
OLIVER	Peace
OSCAR	Divine spear
OTTO	Wealthy
PATRICK	Noble, patrician
PAUL	Little
PERRY	Pear tree
PETER	Rock
PHILIP	Lover of horses
RANDOLPH	Protected; advised by wolves
RAOUL	Helpful commander
RICHARD	Wealthy and powerful
ROBERT	Of bright, shining fame
RYAN	Laughing
SALVADOR	Of the Savior
SAMUEL	Name of God
SANCHO	Gallant companion
SCOTT	A Scotsman
SEAN	God's gracious gift
SHELLEY	From the ledge
SIDNEY	Follower of Saint Denis
SPENCER	Storekeeper
STANLEY	Pride of the camp
STEPHEN	Crown, garland

STEWART	Keeper of the estate
TERENCE	Tender
THEODORE	Gift of God
THOMAS	The twin
TIMOTHY	Honoring God
TODD	The fox
VAN	From
VICTOR	The conqueror
WALTER	Powerful warrior
WARNER	Protecting warrior
WAYNE	Wagon maker
WILLIAM	Determined protector
YALE	The yielder

THE SEVEN DAYS OF THE WEEK

MONDAY
(wear pearls on Monday)

"As Monday does, so goes all the week" is an old proverb which many believe. Don't move on a Monday, although Monday is a lucky day, a day of happiness and peace.

TUESDAY
(wear rubies on Tuesday)

Tuesdays are generally unlucky days. They often bring quarrels and lawsuits. Tuesdays are good days for marriage and to begin a new business deal.

WEDNESDAY
(wear sapphires on Wednesday)

The sun shines on Wednesday; but if it doesn't, there will be a terrible storm. Wednesdays are very lucky days; in fact, they are considered the best day of the week to be born.

THURSDAY
(wear garnets on Thursday)

Some believe that Thursdays are very unlucky days and that there is only one good hour (the one before dawn) on any given Thursday. But it's a good day to perform difficult tasks.

FRIDAY
(wear emeralds on Friday)

Considered the most unlucky day of the week; nothing good can happen on a Friday. Don't start anything on a Friday. So many bad things have happened on Fridays that there's no use tempting fate. (*See* FRIDAY)

SATURDAY
(wear diamonds on Saturday)

An unlucky day; nothing new should be begun on a Saturday. A new moon on a Saturday is unlucky and brings trouble. The sun will shine on a Saturday, even if only for a moment.

SUNDAY
(wear yellow stones)

Sunday is a lucky day, a favorite for weddings. It is considered a good day to be born. If you sneeze on a Sunday before breakfast you'll be in love forever.

SPORTING SUPERSTITIONS

AUTO RACING

If a (male) driver eats peanuts or talks to a woman before a race, he can expect trouble during the race.

A woman in the garage area was taboo until 1971, when two female reporters got a court order to allow them in the pit area during the Indianapolis 500.

BASEBALL

Spit into your hands before picking up a baseball bat for good luck.

A player who changes bats after two strikes will be struck out.

A piece of chewing gum stuck to the top of a baseball cap brings good luck.

Crossing bats on a baseball field will bring bad luck to the batter.

Seventh-inning stretch is an attempt by fans to bring good luck to their team by invoking the magic of the number seven. (*See* SEVEN)

BASKETBALL

The player who makes the last basket during warm-ups will do well during the game. Some believe this superstition works the other way: The player who makes the last basket at warm-up will do very badly during the game.

BOWLING

Don't fill in the score of a person who is having a string of strikes until that string has broken.

If a split occurs (that doesn't turn into a spare), the superstitious bowler will mark a heavy vertical line—called a fence—after the frame, to prevent that sort of unlucky split from happening again during the game.

GOLF

When you are teeing off, you should place a ball with the trade name or number facing up or the hole is lost.

The word socket used on the golf course, is considered bad luck by players.

All numbered balls, over the number four, are considered bad luck.

HORSE RACING

Gray horses and horses with four white hooves are unlucky.

If a photo is taken of a jockey and a horse together before they've ridden the race, they'll lose.

It is believed that a jockey's boot must never touch the floor before it is on the jockey's foot or it will slow the jockey down.

It is unlucky for the jockey to drop the whip before a race.

HORSES (NOT RACING)

Spotted horses or ones with patches of color are believed to have magical gifts.

Bells and brass disks are attached to harnesses to ward off the evil eye and other evil spirits. Another method used to protect against witches and the evil eye is placing a piece of red cloth on the forehead of the horse.

MOUNTAINEERING

Mountaintops are where the gods live, and if you attempt to climb up to their homes, evil spirits will attack you. This was a widespread belief during early times. In 1387, six clergymen climbed Mount Pilatus (in the Swiss Alps) to attempt to destroy the superstition that Pontius Pilate's spirit lived on top and that it took revenge on anyone who disturbed it. Their climb was completely successful—except that they were arrested as soon as they arrived at the bottom of the mountain!

PRIZEFIGHTING (BOXING)

If a fighter carries a pickle during a fight, the fighter will get knocked out!

TENNIS

It's bad luck to hold three tennis balls in your hand while serving.

TRACK RACING

Never let anyone step across your legs before a race.
Never let a pole come between you and a fellow competitor—both people must pass the pole on the same side or there will be unhappy results for both.

TREES AND THEIR MEANINGS

APPLE	Temptation
ASH	Grandeur
ASPEN	Grieving
BAY	Glory
BARBERRY	Sharpness
BIRCH	Meek and graceful
BOX	Stoic
CEDAR OF LEBANON	Strong and constant
CHERRY	Education
(White)	Deception
CHESTNUT	Luxury
DOGWOOD	Durable
EBONY	Blackness
ELDER	Zealousness
ELM	Dignity
FIR (Scotch)	Elevate
HAWTHORN	Hope
HAZEL	Reconciliation
LEMON	Zest
LINDEN (Lime)	Conjugal love
LOCUST	Elegance
MAPLE	Reserve
MULBERRY	
(White)	Wisdom
(Black)	I will not survive you

OAK	Hospitality
ORANGE	Generosity
PEACH BLOSSOM	I am your captive
PEAR	Comfort
POPLAR (Black)	Courage
(White)	Time
WEEPING	
WILLOW	Mourning

LANGUAGE OF FLOWERS
(as devised about 200 years ago)

See also CHARTS, Flowers

ACACIA	Friendship
(Pink)	Elegance
(Rose)	Platonic love
(Yellow)	Secret love
ACANTHUS	The fine arts
ALOE	Grief, bitterness, associated with religious superstitions
AMARYLLIS	Pride, haughtiness
ANEMONE (Garden)	Forsaken
(Meadow)	Sickness
(Wood)	Forlornness
ASTER	Variety
(Double)	I share your sentiments
(Single)	I will think of it
AZALEA	Temperance
BACHELOR'S BUTTON	Love and marriage
BLUEBELL	Constant kindness
BOUQUET OF FLOWERS	Gallantry
BUTTERCUP	Cheerful but ungrateful
CARNATION	Fascination; woman's love
(Striped)	Refusal
(Yellow)	Disdain
CHAMOMILE	Energy even when troubled

CHRYSANTHEMUMS	Cheerful even when troubled
(Red)	I love
(White)	Truth
(Yellow)	Slighted love
COLUMBINE	Folly
(Purple)	Resolute
(Red)	Anxious
CORNFLOWER	Delicate
CROCUS	Do not abuse
(Spring)	Youthful hope
DAFFODIL	Regard
(Great Yellow)	Chivalry
DAHLIA	Instability
DAISY	Innocence
(Double)	Participation
(Garden)	I share your sentiments
DANDELION	Love's oracle
DEAD LEAVES	Sadness, melancholy
FERN	Sincerity
FLEUR-DE-LIS	Flame
FORGET-ME-NOT	Remember; true love
FRANKINCENSE	The incense of a faithful heart
GATHERED FLOWERS	We will die together
GERANIUM	Gentility
(Dark)	Melancholy
(Rose or Pink)	Preference
(Scarlet)	Comforting; stupidity and folly
(Wild)	Steadfast piety
GOLDENROD	Careful encouragement
GRASS	Useful
HIBISCUS	Delicate beauty
HOLLY	Foresight
HOLLYHOCK	Fruitfulness
(White)	Female ambition
HONEYSUCKLE (Coral)	Color of my fate
(French)	Rustic beauty
(Monthly; Woodbine)	Bond of love; I'll answer with care

(Wild)	Inconstancy in love
HYACINTH	Sport
(Blue)	Constant
IRIS	My compliments; I have a message for you.
(German)	Ardor
(Yellow)	Flame
IVY	Friendship, fidelity
JASMINE (Cape)	Transport of joy
(Carolina)	Separation
(Indian)	I attach myself to you
(Spanish)	Sensuality
(White)	Amiability
(Yellow)	Grace and elegance
JONQUIL	I want you to love me
LAUREL (Bay)	Glory
(Common)	Perfidy
(Mountain)	Ambition, glory
LAVENDER	Distrust
LILAC (Field)	Humility
(Purple)	The first signs of love
(White)	Purity, modesty
LILY (Day)	Coquetry
(White)	Purity and sweetness
(Yellow)	Lies and gaiety
LILY OF THE VALLEY	Return of happiness
LOTUS	Eloquence
LOVE-IN-IDLENESS	Love at first sight
MAGNOLIA	Love of nature
MANDRAKE ROOT	Horror
MARIGOLD	Grief, pain, and anger
MISTLETOE	Surmount all obstacles
MOSS	Maternal love
MYRTLE	Love
NARCISSUS	Egotism, self-esteem
ORANGE BLOSSOM	You're as pure as you are lovely; chastity

PEA (Sweet)	Departure
PEONY	Shame
POPPY	Fading pleasures
(Red)	Consolation
(Scarlet)	Fantastic extravagance
(White)	Sleep helps everything
PRIMROSE	Early youth
RHODODENDRON	Danger
ROSE	Love and beauty
(Bridal)	Happy love
(Burgundy)	Unconscious beauty
(Cabbage)	Ambassador of love
(Carolina)	Love is dangerous
(Damask)	Brilliant complexion
(Deep red)	Bashful
(Full red)	Beauty
(Full white)	I am worthy of you
(Musk)	Capricious beauty
(White)	Silence
(Yellow)	Jealousy, unfaithfulness
(Red and white together)	Unity
SHAMROCK	Lightheartedness, Ireland
SNAPDRAGON	Presumption
SUNFLOWER	Adoration
(Tall)	Haughtiness
TUBEROSE	Dangerous pleasures
TULIP	Fame
(Red)	Declaration of love
(Yellow)	Hopeless love
(Variegated)	Beautiful eyes
VIOLET (Blue)	Faithfulness in love
(Dame)	You are the queen of coquettes
(Purple)	You occupy my thoughts
(Sweet)	Modesty
(Wild)	Love in idleness
WILDFLOWER	Fidelity in misfortune
ZINNIA	Thoughts of absent friends

WEDDING ANNIVERSARY GIFTS

FIRST	Paper
SECOND	Cotton
THIRD	Leather
FOURTH	Fruits and flowers (or linen)
FIFTH	Wood
SIXTH	Sugar and candy (or iron)
SEVENTH	Woolens and copper
EIGHTH	Rubber and bronze
NINTH	Pottery and willow
TENTH	Tin
ELEVENTH	Steel
TWELFTH	Silk and fine linen
THIRTEENTH	Lace
FOURTEENTH	Ivory
FIFTEENTH	Crystal
TWENTIETH	China
TWENTY-FIFTH	Silver
THIRTIETH	Pearl
THIRTY-FIFTH	Coral
FORTIETH	Ruby
FORTY-FIFTH	Sapphire
FIFTIETH	Gold
FIFTY-FIFTH	Emerald
SIXTIETH and SEVENTY-FIFTH	Diamond

BIBLIOGRAPHY

Ballou, Maturin M. *Treasury of Thought, A.*, Cambridge: Houghton Mifflin Co. (Boston)/Riverside Press, 1896.

Bartlett, John. *Bartlett's Familiar Quotations.* New York: Little, Brown & Co., 1955.

Batchelor, Julie Forsyth and Claudia DeLys. *Superstitious? Here's Why!* New York: Harcourt, Brace and World, Inc., 1954.

Benet, William Rose. *Reader's Encyclopedia, The.* 2nd ed. New York: Thomas Y. Crowell Co., 1965.

Bowser, James W., ed. *6,000 Names for Baby.* New York: Dell/Ivy Books, 1978.

Brooks, Daniel Fitzgerald. *Numerology.* New York: Franklin Watts, 1978.

Burnam, Tom. *Dictionary of Mis-Information, The.* New York: Thomas Y. Crowell Co., 1975.

Coffin, Margaret M. *Death in Early America,* New York: Thomas Nelson, Inc., 1976.

Complete Book of Astrology, Horoscope and Dreams. New York: Modern Promotions, 1979.

Cowan, Lore. *Are You Superstitious?* New York: Apex, 1969.

DeLys, Claudia. *Treasury of American Superstitions, A.* New York: Philosophical Library, Inc., 1958.

DeLys, Claudia. *Treasury of Superstitions, A.* New York: Philosophical Library, Inc., 1957.

Espy, Willard R. *Another Almanac of Words at Play.* New York: Clarkson N. Potter, 1980.

Evans, Bergen. *Comfortable Words.* New York: Random House, 1959.

Evans, Bergen. *Dictionary of Quotations.* New York: Avenel Books, 1978.

Farmer, Penelope. *Beginnings.* New York: Atheneum, 1979.

Funk & Wagnall's Standard Dictionary of Folklore, Myth and Legend. New York: Funk & Wagnall, 1972.

Funk, Charles Earle. Heavens To Betsy! New York: Harper & Brothers, 1955.

Garden, Nancy. *Witches.* New York: J.B. Lippincott Co., 1975.

Garrison, Webb. *How it Started.* New York: Abingdon Press, 1972.

Gray, Eden. *Tarot Revealed, The.* New York: Bell Publishing Co., 1960.

Greenway, Kate and Jean Marsh. *Illuminated Language of Flowers.* New York: Holt, Rhinehart & Winston, 1978.

Heaps, Willard A. *Superstition!* New York: Thomas Nelson, Inc., 1972.

Helfman, Elizabeth S. *Signs and Symbols Around the World.* New York: Lothrop, Lee & Shepard, Co., 1967.

Hollingsworth, Buckner. *Flower Chronicles.* New Jersey: Rutgers University Press, 1958.

Huggett, Richard. *Supernatural on Stage.* New York: Taplinger Publishing Co., 1975.

Krythe, Maymie R. *All About the Months.* New York: Harper & Row Publishers, Inc., 1966.

Lawson, J. Gilchrist. *World's Best Conundrums and Riddles of All Ages, The.* New York: Harper & Brothers, 1924.

Lewis, Linda Rannells. *Birthdays.* New York: Little, Brown & Co. (An Atlantic Monthly Press Book), 1976.

Louis, David. *More Fascinating Facts.* New York: Ridge Press/ Crown Publishing Co., 1976.

Mann, Peggy. *Telltale Line, The.* New York: Macmillan Publishing Co., 1976.

Maple, Eric. *Superstition and the Superstitious.* New York: A.S. Barnes & Co., 1972.

Mercatante, Anthony S. *Who's Who in Egyptian Mythology.* New York: Clarkson N. Potter, Inc., 1978.

Morris, William and Mary. *Dictionary of Word and Phrase Origins.* New York: Harper & Row Publishers, 1962.

Morrison, Lillian, (compiled by). *Touch Blue.* New York: Thomas Y. Crowell Co., 1958.

Myers, Robert. *Celebrations.* New York: Doubleday & Co., Inc., 1972.

Powell, Claire. *Meaning of Flowers, The.* London: Jupiter Books, 1977.

Rachleff, Owen S. *Secrets of Superstition, The.* New York: Doubleday & Co., Inc., 1976.

Radford, Edwin. *Encyclopedia of Superstition.* London: Hutchinson, 1961.

Reader's Digest's American Folklore and Legend. Pleasantville, New York: Reader's Digest Association, 1978.

Reader's Digest's Stories Behind Everyday Things. Pleasantville, New York: Reader's Digest Association, 1980.

Rosten, Leo. *Joys of Yiddish, The.* New York: McGraw-Hill Book Co., 1968.

Ruoff, Henry W. *Century Book of Facts, The.* King-Richardson Co., 1902.

Sarnoff, Jane and Reynold Ruffins. *Take Warning!* New York: Charles Scribner's and Sons, 1978.

Schwartz, Alvin. *Cross Your Fingers, Spit in Your Hat.* New York: J.B. Lippincott Co., 1974.

Seymour, John. *Gardner's Delight.* New York: Harmony Books, 1979.

Stevenson, Burton. *Home Book of Proverbs, Maxims and Familiar Phrases, The.* New York: Macmillan Co., 1948.

Stimpson, George. *Book About a Thousand Things, A.* New York: Harper and Brothers, 1946.

Sullivan, George. *Sports Superstitions.* New York: Coward, McCann & Geoghegan, Inc., 1978.

Van Druten, John. *Bell, Book and Candle.* New York: Random House, Inc., 1951.

Vogel, Malvina (compiled and edited by). *Big Book of Amazing Facts, The.* New York: Playmore, Inc./Waldman Publishing Corp., 1980.

Wagner, Edward A. *Sun-Sign Handbook, The.* New York: Dell/Ivy Book, 1979.

Wallechinsky, David and Irving Wallace. *People's Almanac #2, The.* New York: Bantam Books, Inc., 1978.

Zolar's Horoscope and Lucky Number Dream Book. New York: Prestige Books, Inc., 1980.